A SPIRITUAL CALENDAR

A SELECTION OF THOUGHTS FOR EVERY DAY IN THE YEAR

FROM THE WORKS AND LETTERS OF
ANTONIO ROSMINI
FOUNDER OF THE INSTITUTE OF CHARITY

NEW YORK, CINCINNATI, CHICAGO
BENZIGER BROTHERS
PRINTERS TO THE PUBLISHERS OF
HOLY APOSTOLIC SEE BENZIGER'S MAGAZINE

1911

Imprimatur
✠ RICARDUS, *Epus. Mediob.*
die 8 *Octob.*, 1911.

NOTE.

This little book is in the main a translation of the "Calendarietto Spirituale," compiled by the late Right Rev. Aloysius Lanzoni, Fifth Provost General of the Institute of Charity. A scriptural text, bearing on the subject treated of in the passage quoted, has been added to the sentence selected for each day. The book has been prepared to serve in the first instance for the year 1909, but the reader will easily be able to make the few changes which are required in order that the sentences may accord with the moveable feasts in subsequent years.

GEORGE ELSON, I.C.

Christmas 1908.

SPIRITUAL CALENDAR

JANUARY

1. CIRCUMCISION. Let us begin a new life with the New Year. Returning to God with circumcised hearts, free from wilful faults, let us cling to brighter hopes and to those thoughts which comfort the soul of the true penitent even amidst his tears of repentance and feelings of sorrow. (Sermons p. 63.)

For in Christ Jesus neither circumcision availeth anything nor uncircumcision, but a new creature. (Galatians vi. 15.)

2. The recollection of God's presence, assiduous prayer, purity of intention in our actions, and the practice of good works are sure means of preserving and enhancing the interior spirit. (Pedagogics vol. ii. p. 319.)

Walk before Me and be perfect. (Genesis xvii. 1.)

3. A man who bears in mind that God is everywhere present beholding his every action, will hardly ever sin, conscious as he is of having at every moment a companion of infinite dignity, authority, justice and sanctity. (Christian Education Book III. chap. ii. No. 4.)

Blessed are all they that fear the Lord, that walk in His ways. (Psalm cxxvii. 1.)

4. Pray always, not merely at stated times, and have a stock of ejaculatory prayers to be said often during the day. These should be adapted to the end you have in view, and to the various circumstances in which you are placed. (Christian Education Book I. chap. vi. No. 2.)

We ought always to pray, and not to faint. (St. Luke xviii. 1.)

5. Our Lord's maxim that every one should aim at perfection, and become more and more like to God, should be deeply engraven on your mind. No lawful occupation can hinder this. (Christian Education Book I. chap. xi. No. 4.)

Be you therefore perfect as also your heavenly Father is perfect. (St. Matthew v. 48.)

6. EPIPHANY. To keep holy the Epiphany a Christian should—1st, recall how the Gentiles, of whom the Magi were first and of whom we are descendants, were called by God to the Faith ; 2nd, pray to God that he would vouchsafe to bestow the light of Faith on those nations that have not yet received it ; 3rd, offer himself to God with all that he has, in imitation of the Magi, acknowledging Him as King, God and Man. (Catechism No. 679.)

The Gentiles shall walk in Thy light, and kings in the brightness of Thy rising. (Isaias ix. 3.)

7. One of the causes which facilitated the preaching of the Gospel, was undoubtedly the consciousness men had of their own corruption, and the urgent need they felt of reform in order to save the very fabric of human society which was tottering to its fall under a crushing weight of wickedness. (Theodicy No. 528. Note.)

The people that walked in darkness have

seen a great light: to them that dwelt in the region of the shadow of death, light is risen. (Isaias ix. 2.)

8. Only the Wisdom of God was able to discover in the most degraded of men a disposition suitable for the reception of His benefits, and to make use of human infirmity to erect, as it were, a new edifice of Divine workmanship upon frail and worthless human nature. (Theodicy No. 530.)
But the foolish things of the world hath God chosen, that He may confound the wise; and the weak things of the world hath God chosen that He may confound the strong; and the base things of the world, and the things that are contemptible hath God chosen, and things that are not, that He might bring to nought things that are; that no flesh should glory in His sight. (1 Corinthians i. 27, 28, 29.)

9. Jesus Christ has no need of us: His call is pure mercy. A man may lose his soul through one day's delay in corresponding to divine grace. (Letters 1175.)
To-day if you shall hear His voice, harden not your hearts. (Psalm xciv. 8.)

10. The love God bears and always has borne towards mankind is not only the cause of love in the hearts of those who do love Him, but also renders it possible to those who do not yet love Him. (History of Love Book III. chap i. No 2.)

Let us therefore love God, because God first hath loved us. (1 St. John iv. 19.)

11. How great a gain is a soul saved for our Lord! But this is not the work of man whose words can only reach the ear: it is God who changes the heart. (Letters 592.)

Therefore neither he that planteth is anything, nor he that watereth, but God that giveth the increase. (1 Corinthians iii. 7.)

12. God usually sends preachers of the Gospel to the nations when He sees they are ripe to receive the message: "Lift up your eyes, and see the countries for they are white already to harvest." (St. John iv. 35.) . . . . Every nation enters the Church only when it has reached that point of maturity which is entirely hidden from men and known only to the infinite wisdom of God . . . . One is called at the third hour, another at the sixth, one at the ninth hour, another at the eleventh. (Letters 4977.)

The kingdom of heaven is like to a householder who went out . . . . to hire labourers into his vineyard. (St. Matthew xx. 1.)

13. All individuals who compose the human race, but principally all Christians, can save their souls if only they have the hope and the will, since obduracy of heart is found in those only who no longer will to be saved or who despair, so that no one can say with truth, "I wish to be saved, but it is impossible." (1 Theodicy No. 997.)

For this is good and acceptable in the sight of God our Saviour, who will have all men to be saved, and to come to the knowledge of the truth. (1 Timothy ii. 3, 4.)

14. To fear God with that just fear, which leads man to refrain from evil, is the beginning of all good. (The Magnificat Explained No. 16.)

The fear of the Lord is a fountain of life,

to decline from the ruin of death. (Proverbs xiv. 27.)

15. Our faith is the basis of the whole fabric of religion, and a Christian is bound to take every precaution for keeping his faith pure and unalloyed. We must not let errors against the Faith sink into our minds even materially,—a thing which may happen without actual malice by merely reading a contaminated book . . . . I hope that I am not scrupulous, but in matters of faith laxity is fatal. The day may come when what you read now might cause you great disquietude. We all have need of peace of mind. (Letters 751.)

For I say . . . . to all that are among you, not to be more wise than it behoveth to be wise, but to be wise unto sobriety, and according as God hath divided to every one the measure of faith. (Romans xii. 3.)

16. Even in this solitude into which God has led me, where everything helps to uplift the soul to Him, where neither the pomp nor the falsehood of the world can penetrate; even here we are in danger's way, even here we have the battle with self and with the devil, and conquer we cannot unless by taking to ourselves the shield of faith, the helmet of salvation, and the sword of the spirit, which is the word of God. In every deed the life of man on earth is a warfare. (Letters 786.)

For our wrestling is not against flesh and blood, but against principalities and powers, against the rulers of the world of this darkness, against the spirits of wickedness in the high places. (Ephesians vi. 12.)

17. THE HOLY NAME OF JESUS. Well did St. Bernard say that no book had any charm for him which did not contain the most lovable of all names, the Name of of Jesus! So indeed it ought to be: all that is not signed and seasoned with this Name should be insipid to Christians. (Letters 571.)

For which cause God also hath exalted Him, and hath given Him a name which is above all names, that in the name of Jesus every knee should bow, of those that are in heaven, on earth, and under the earth. (Philippians ii. 9, 10.)

18. We must be persuaded that to love

truth is a duty, the first and foremost of duties, the source of all others. (Treatise on Moral Conscience. 2nd Edition p. 235.)

We can do nothing against the truth, but for the truth. (2 Corinthians xiii. 8.)

19. As a rule the vices which lurk within our souls and corrupt them, as a worm eats away the wood, are those which spring from self-love. (Letters 4176.)

Every way of a man seemeth right to himself, but the Lord weigheth the hearts. (Proverbs xxi. 2.)

20. Even the desire of good has its illusions, but you can never be deceived by the submission of your own judgment and the renunciation even of things which, though good in appearance, are not comformable to obedience. (Letters 4236.)

As children of obedience, not fashioned according to the former desires of your ignorance, but according to Him that hath called you, who is holy. (1 St. Peter i. 14, 15.)

21. Our God is the God of truth, and our Master is the very Truth. The world indeed cares little for truth, and consequently but little for God. (Letters 4336.)

Doing the truth in charity, we may in all things grow up in Him who is the Head even Christ. (Ephesians iv. 15.)

22. I am firmly persuaded that there never was a time in which men of sacrifice were more needed than the present day; and perhaps such men were never before so scarce. (Letters 2884.)

For all seek the things that are their own, not the things that are Jesus Christ's. (Philippians ii. 21.)

23. OUR LADY'S ESPOUSALS. Did any man rule over Mary? Joseph was legally her spouse, but we cannot doubt that he revered her as his Lady and did not regard her as subject to himself. To whom then was Mary subject but to Him of whom she declared herself the handmaid: " Behold the handmaid of the Lord?" (Letters 5071.)

He that is mighty hath done great things to me, and holy is His name. (St. Luke i. 49.)

24. As long as we live on this earth

we have unfortunately a twofold being, the spirit and the flesh, and these two are ever striving for the mastery. Howbeit the combat makes for victory, and victory wins the crown. (Letters 4607.)

The flesh lusteth against the spirit, and the spirit against the flesh, for these are contrary one to another. (Galatians v. 17.)

25. CONVERSION OF ST. PAUL. Great conversions seem to have for their end, not merely the salvation of the soul that is gained by each of them (although no one could adequately estimate the value of that one soul in the sight of God), but also the salvation of many others. Thus, for example, Saul, through his conversion, became the Apostle of the Gentiles; St. Augustine became the Doctor of Grace; the Good Thief, Magdalene and other sinners whose conversions are recorded in the Gospel became luminous examples to all the world, and striking proofs of God's mercy for all time. (Theodicy No. 533.)

Wisdom reacheth therefore from end to end mightily, and ordereth all things sweetly. (Wisdom viii. 1.)

26. In the spiritual life consolation is no sign of progress, and aridity is not a sign that we are losing ground. (Letters 2673.)
Thou visitest him early in the morning, and Thou provest him suddenly. (Job. vii. 18.)

27. If, by God's grace we first preach to ourselves, we shall effect our own conversion, and then shall we verily begin to be powerful in word and to produce fruit in our neighbour. What we impart to them must be out of our own heart, and of our own love. (Pedagogics Vol. II. p. 275.)
But I chastise my body, and bring it into subjection, lest perhaps, when I have preached to others, I myself should become a cast-away. (1 Corinthians ix. 27.)

28. Gentleness is a most delicate virtue. A slight raising of the voice, a hasty gesture, a sharp glance, a smile, a touch of irony, the tone of voice, the merest trifle may suffice to wound this virtue, for it is as sensitive as self-love, and that is of all things the most sensitive. (Letters 1849.)
Learn of Me, because I am meek and humble of heart. (St. Matthew xi. 29.)

29. St. Francis of Sales used to say that "self-love is a great mischief-maker": I would say the same of the imagination, which is often in league with self-love. (Letters 1186.)

The imagination and thought of man's heart are prone to evil from his youth. (Genesis viii. 21.)

30. Permit me to beg and entreat you to hold aloof, especially at the present time, from all parties, and to be content with the sound doctrine of the Catholic Church. This is the doctrine of God: all else is the doctrine of men. What is it that we have in view in our study of religion? Is it our salvation or the gratification of curiosity? Salvation is found in the true doctrine of the Church: curiosity and self-love find pleasure in party tenets. The tenets of a party are always tainted by the vices of the men who form that party. The doctrine of the Church is pure; it does not produce confusion and distress of mind because it does not rouse the passions. (Letters 751.)

For there shall be a time when they will not endure sound doctrine; but according to their own desires they will heap to themselves teachers, having itching ears, and will indeed turn away their hearing from the truth, but will be turned unto fables. (2 Timothy iv. 3, 4).

31. Be very sure of this: the visible world is one continual delusion. Cherish unbounded love for things invisible, virtue, grace, and the tranquil enjoyment of heavenly gifts. (Letters 6167.)
Be zealous for the better gifts. (1 Corinthians xii, 31.)

FEBRUARY

1. St. Ignatius, M. By all means let us offer ourselves to our Lord and to His love, without imagining, however, that we have already become His victims.... Let us imitate St. Ignatius the Martyr. It was only on hearing the roar of the lions about to devour him, that he exclaimed, full of joy: "Now do I begin to be a disciple of Christ." (Letters 5261.)

My heart is ready, O God, my heart is ready. (Psalm cvii. 2.)

2. Purification of B.V.M. Mary would comply with the law of Purification, because she did not wish to make known to men her Divine Maternity, nor would she scandalise them by appearing to be disobedient to the law. (Catechism No. 687.)

And after the days of her purification according to the law of Moses were accomplished, they carried Him to Jerusalem, to present Him to the Lord. (St. Luke ii. 22.)

3. Let your conduct be always characterized by the simplicity and prudence of the Spirit of God, to the exclusion of all human artifice, trickery or dissimulation. (Letters 730.)

Be ye therefore wise as serpents and simple as doves. (St. Matthew x. 16.)

4. Oh, how much more precious is the solitude of the heart than that of the walls of a monastery! We must erect within us walls of fire, so that nothing may enter therein but the Spirit of God who is fire. These walls are the love of God and of our neighbour. (Letters 6249.)

I will lead her into the wilderness, and I will speak to her heart. (Osee ii. 14.)

5. It is but too true that the breath of the world contaminates. It is pestilential, and we inhale it unconsciously. (Letters 1175.)

All that is in the world is the concupiscence of the flesh and the concupiscence of the eyes and the pride of life, which is not of the Father, but is of the world. (1 St. John ii. 16.)

6. At any cost let us do our duty; at any cost be faithful to God; let all else perish provided we advance in perfection and the imitation of Jesus Christ, who entered into glory by means of suffering. (Letters 5753.)

Be thou faithful unto death; and I will give thee the crown of life. (Apocalypse ii. 10.)

7. Let us shun the spirit of the world, which is a spirit of dissipation and death, let us adopt the spirit of Holy Church, a spirit of penance, recollection, and life. We are all sworn to this . . . . for we are all Christians. (Sermons p. 74.)

Love not the world, nor the things which are in the world. If any man love the world the charity of the Father is not in him. (1 St. John ii. 15.)

8. The study of perfection consists in always keeping our thoughts and affections on what is eternal; if we fix them on transitory things our resolutions can have no stability. (Letters 5337.)

While we look not at the things which are seen, but at the things which are not seen.

For the things which are seen are temporal; but the things which are not seen, are eternal. (2 Corinthians iv. 18.)

9. This is the great secret of the spiritual life, to keep the thought of God and of Eternity ever present to our mind, and to consider all else as nothing. Thus shall we fulfil the precept of Christ: "Abide in me, and I in you . . . . for without me you can do nothing." (Letters 5504.)
Abide in My love. (St. John xv. 9.)

10. I recommend you to cultivate cheerfulness and a holy mirth; beware of ill humour. Remember the honey of St. Francis of Sales, one drop of which caught more flies than a barrel of vinegar. (Letters 2217.)
A joyful mind maketh age flourishing; a sorrowful spirit drieth up the bones. (Proverbs xvii. 22.)

11. I have often wondered why our Blessed Lady did not tell St. Joseph of the apparition of the Angel, and I think it was because she could give no proof of it and she was so humble that she did not feel her mere word to be a warrant for believing. (Letters 1066.)

He hath regarded the humility of His handmaid. (St. Luke i. 48.)

12. Then indeed we hope in God, when we feel that we have nothing to rely on in ourselves. We have need of experience. The knowledge acquired by the mind is too cold and ineffectual of itself, without that blessed experimental knowledge which was possessed by the Saints and by Christ Himself according to the Apostle: " He learned obedience by the things He suffered." (Letters 684.)

What doth he know that hath not been tried? . . . . He that hath no experience knoweth little, and he that hath been experienced in many things, multiplieth prudence. (Ecclesiasticus xxxiv. 9, 10.)

13. God can do all things, and He is the more wonderful the more He works alone. When I think I see God working, so to say, more of Himself, then I have greater courage, as His Will seems to be thus more manifest. (Letters 703.)

For Thou art great and dost wonderful things: Thou art God alone. Conduct me, O Lord, in Thy way, and I will walk in Thy truth. (Psalm lxxxv. 10, 11.)

14. Let us rest in God: a heart that looks to God and leans on Him finds there such comfort and such strength that not only the multitude, but also those who pass for philosophers, deem it incredible and almost miraculous. (Letters 97.)

I set the Lord always in my sight, for He is at my right hand, that I be not moved. Therefore my heart hath been glad, and my tongue hath rejoiced: moreover my flesh also shall rest in hope. (Psalm xv. 8, 9.)

15. It always seems to me a good thing to reflect on what is being suffered at every moment in all parts of the world; how many there are struggling in the agony of death; how many are battling with the fiercest temptations, how many are enduring a martyrdom of interior suffering. We do not know individually those who are tried in so many ways; but even to know how many there are continually suffering in this vale of tears is enough to make us acknowledge that our Lord treats us very gently in comparison, and to make us grateful to Him for it. (Letters 5164.)

Many are the afflictions of the just; but out of them all will the Lord deliver them. (Psalm xxxiii. 20.)

16. It is peculiar to charity, not only to compassionate our neighbour, but also to look at him in the most favourable light. Even should it happen that, on account of this benevolent disposition, some error of judgment should occur, it is still a fortunate error, since it brings merit to the mistaken person and helps to union amongst men. (Letters 7232.)

And be ye kind one to another, merciful, forgiving one another, even as God hath forgiven you in Christ. (Ephesians iv. 32.)

17. The hypocrite, as Jesus Christ observes (Matthew vi), is always melancholy and sad. He hides the gloomy remorse of his heart under the appearance of sternness and rigour by which he aspires to be accounted austere and virtuous. On the other hand nothing manifests the truly sincere spirit of the saints so clearly as their cheerfulness; it carries with it the evidence of truth. (Apologetics p. 104.)

Every one as he hath determined in his heart, not with sadness or of necessity, for God loveth a cheerful giver. (2 Corinthians ix. 7.)

18. As long as we live in this world, our mind is but too often filled with a multitude of notions which are false though they appear to be pious, and our heart is filled with vain and useless desires which are religious only in seeming. No, no, let us rid our minds of these trammels, and our hearts of these vain delusions, let us bring ourselves to that simplicity of thought and feeling which is taught by the Gospel. (Letters 1373.)

Amen I say to you, unless you be converted, and become as little children, you shall not enter into the kingdom of heaven. (St. Matthew xviii. 3.)

19. The light that comes from God and the reasoning that proceeds from this light are *simple*, and in no way involved, long and unending. (Letters 4807.)

The light of thy body is thy eye. If thy eye be single thy whole body shall be lightsome. (St. Matthew vi. 22.)

20.* God alone knows the times and the moments, and you remember my motto: It is good to wait with silence for the salvation of God. This is the ruling principle of all my actions, and I have had the words written over the door of my cell at Monte Calvario. (Letters 5729.)

It is not for you to know the times or moments which the Father hath put in His own power. (Acts i. 7.)

21. Do not think that Holy Church is opposed to joy and innocent amusement; howbeit, she would have our mirth to be reasonable and not senseless. Man does not really rejoice, except when he derives his pleasure from true and solid motives. When he lacks these, his merriment is

---

*On February 20th, 1828, Rosmini took up his abode at Monte Calvario, Domodossola, and began the foundation of the Institute of Charity. (Ed.)

foolish and void of taste, and sorrow founded in truth is to be preferred to it. (Sermons p. 67.)

Rejoice in the Lord always; again, I say, rejoice. . . . . The Lord is nigh. (Philippians iv. 4, 5.)

22. Let us cultivate a holy cheerfulness, not a boisterous, worldly joy, which dissipates the spirit, but that gentle and tranquil gladness which springs chiefly from a pure conscience, from the grace of the Holy Ghost shed abroad in our hearts, and from resignation to the Divine Will. (Letters 510.)

The fruit of the Spirit is charity, joy, peace. (Galatians v. 22.)

23. Worldlings either believe or strive to make others believe that a Christian life is altogether sad, painful, gloomy and bereft of all comfort and happiness. . . . . . Nothing can be more fatal, nothing falser than this baneful error. (Sermons pp. 255, 256.)

Religiousness shall keep and justify the heart, it shall give joy and gladness. (Ecclesiasticus i. 18.)

24. Sorrow for sin means a firm resolve to avoid it and to do all possible good, not a feeling of dejection, sadness, melancholy, or a tendency to discouragement. (Letters 4777.)

Rend your hearts, and not your garments, and turn to the Lord your God; for He is gracious and merciful, patient and rich in mercy, and ready to repent of the evil. (Joel ii. 13.)

25. One single sin, one single offence against God is enough to make one weep a thousand years. A thousand years do I say? Nay even to burn for all eternity. (Letters 4959.)

Who can understand sins? From my secret ones cleanse me, O Lord, and from those of others spare thy servant. (Psalm xviii. 13, 14.)

26. God makes His servants experience an inexpressible sweetness and heavenly delight, even in the sacrifice of the vain and transitory things which they offer to Him, so that the follower of Christ, despite his privations and mortifications, is far happier than the worldling . . . . . . Who can describe the sweetness with which God soothes the very tears of penitents? (Sermons p. 256.)

Take up My yoke upon you. . . . . For My yoke is sweet and My burden light. (St. Matthew xi. 29, 30.)

27. If we ask sinners themselves who have returned to God with their whole heart, what language could describe the sweetness of their tears? How delicious a balm soothes all their austerities and penances! And if they sometimes seem pitiless and cruel to themselves, this is because the sufferings and mortifications they offer to God have lost all asperity for them, nay, have became their most cherished treasure, their daily food. A heavenly light gleams in their souls, and by that new light they know God all the more intimately the more they have offended Him; they would almost annihilate themselves in order to restore to Him the honour and love of which they have robbed Him; their only grief is that they cannot do this enough, and that all their affections, all their efforts to love Him are no worthy compensation for that love which they have

denied Him because they are always less than He deserves. (Theodicy No. 374.)

According to the multitude of my sorrows in my heart, Thy comforts have given joy to my soul. (Psalm xciii. 19.)

28. For my own part I consider it a safe maxim and one full of solid hope, to desire Justice, and to renew this desire, this good will unceasingly. This should be done even when we seem to ourselves to fall, and to fall without feeling strength to rise; when we seem to be devoid of charity and weighed down by the burden of our original clay. (Letters 778.)

Lord, all my desire is before Thee, and my groaning is not hidden from Thee. (Psalm xxxvii. 10.)

MARCH

1. Many excuse themselves from the practice of mortification, through fear of injuring their bodily health. This consideration may indeed hold good with regard to excessive mortifications, but not with respect to the many mortifications, both interior and exterior, which are not seriously prejudicial to health, and are often beneficial to it, as experience proves in the case of religious whose lives, albeit penitential and mortified, are well known to be longer than those of other men. (Conferences on Ecclesiastical Duties, viii. 7.)

He that loveth his life shall lose it, and he that hateth his life in this world, keepeth it unto life eternal. (St. John xii. 25.)

2. I quite understand that men shrink from suffering; but how is it possible to escape from that which is to be found everywhere, and which pursues us the more we fly from it? (Letters 6596.)

And all that will live godly in Christ Jesus shall suffer persecution. (2 Timothy iii. 12.)

3. I should like you to desire to merit rather than to enjoy, because Christ in praying to the Father for His disciples said that He asked not that they should be taken out of the world, but only that they should be preserved from evil. (Letters 6645.)

It is a more blessed thing to give than to receive. (Acts xx. 35.)

4. Let us remember that we are placed in this short life to build for ourselves an eternal abode, wherein we shall rest from labour and toil, and where there will be nothing to cause us any more weariness or annoyance. (Letters 6544.)

We have not here a lasting city, but we seek one that is to come. (Hebrews xiii. 14.)

5. With regard to the necessities of the Church we should remain in perfect tranquillity, knowing that Jesus Christ still lives, that to Him all power is given in heaven and on earth, and that nothing happens that is not ordained for His greater glory and more complete triumph. (Letters 663.)

Behold I am with you all days, even to the consummation of the world. (St. Matthew xxviii. 20.)

6. The religious loves his Institute inordinately when he loves it more than the Church, or not in due subordination to the Church . . . . The Church of Jesus Christ alone cannot be loved too much, either absolutely or relatively. (Letters 641.)

As Christ also loved the Church, and delivered Himself up for it. (Ephesians v. 25.)

7. ST. THOMAS AQUINAS. It is charity I want, not learning. I have a great dread of learning, and a boundless love for charity. God grant that learning be not a source of division amongst us! God grant that charity may edify and unite us all in Jesus Christ our Lord, to whom alone be all honour and glory for ever. (Letters 242.)

Knowledge puffeth up, but Charity edifieth. (Corinthians viii. 1.)

8. To love the will of God when all is bright and pleasant is no great love, and one knows not even whether it be love at all; but to love it in adversity is a love pure as refined gold, a love that satisfies the cravings of the soul that suffers lovingly. (Letters 2716.)

In the head of the book it is written of me that I should do Thy will. O my God, I have desired it, and Thy law in the midst of my heart. (Psalm xxxix. 8, 9.)

9. Temporal misfortunes sanctify our hearts, make us more humble, more charitable, and more detached from worldly vanities; nay, even disgusted with them. (Letters 5320.)

Take all that shall be brought upon thee and in thy sorrow endure, and in thy humiliation keep patience. (Ecclesiasticus ii. 4.)

10. The whole study of the Christian life is comprised in these two points: the knowledge of self and the knowledge of God. These produce two opposite effects.

Self-knowledge brings with it fear and discouragement, whilst the knowledge of God, on the contrary, infuses unbounded hope and courage. (Letters 688.)

That you may walk worthy of God, in all things pleasing; being fruitful in every good work, and increasing in the knowledge of God. (Colossians i. 10.)

11. It seems to me that we cannot gauge or measure our hope. As it is grounded on the goodness of God, which is infinite, so must it be likewise without limit, whether we be good or bad. If there be any difference it is the wicked who should hope most, for the poor man has more to hope for from a generous patron than a rich man has, and our Lord is most glorified in His liberality towards the wicked. (Letters 4833.)

For God is compassionate and merciful, and will forgive sins in the day of tribulation: and He is a protector to all that seek Him in truth. (Ecclesiasticus ii. 13.)

12. We must remember that the state of contemplation should not be a state of apathy, but of preparation, a state in which fervour, generosity and grace accumulate, so that we may be ready for the work to which God calls us. We should remain in our seclusion like lions in their lair; whilst leading a contemplative life we should be like a bow bent, like a well-corked vessel of generous wine or any compressed force ready to break forth at the proper time with the greater power. (Letters 1837.)

Therefore take unto you the armour of God, that you may be able to esist in the evil day, and to stand in all things perfect . . . having your feet shod with the preparation of the gospel of peace. (Ephesians vi. 13, 15.)

13. The phrase *to do much* for God certainly requires explanation, in order to take a correct view of the matter and avoid illusion. If by the word *much* many external actions are indicated, or one work rather than another, it may happen that what seems much in the eyes of men is little, and even less than nothing, in the eyes of God. *Much* is never done in the spiritual life, except when what is done is

c

in keeping with the will of God. (Letters 7257.)

And be not conformed to this world, but be reformed in the newness of your mind, that you may prove what is the good, and the acceptable, and the perfect will of God. (Romans xii. 2.)

14. Our own weakness and ignorance are two things that can never be sufficiently understood; they produce self-distrust without discouragement. (Letters 2946).

Keep Thou my soul, and deliver me; I shall not be ashamed, for I have hoped in Thee. (Psalm xxiv. 20.)

15. Sensuality is the passion that most of all lowers and degrades human nature, therefore it should also humble it; yet, as a rule, it has the contrary effect. The dissolute person owns his own weakness, yet at the same time fosters it with pride. (Apologetics p. 63 in Note.)

The wicked man, when he is come into the depth of sins, contemneth; but ignominy and reproach follow him. (Proverbs xviii. 3.)

16. Truly excess in eating and drinking is an irrational and animal passion; nay, worse, for the animal follows its natural instinct in eating, whilst man breaks the very laws of nature and instinct, to indulge some artificially-acquired taste: therefore he has all the grossness of a beast together with all the malice of a man. (Conferences on Ecclestiasical Duties viii. 13.)

He that loveth good cheer shall be in want. (Proverbs xxi. 17.)

17. When hunger reminds us of the need of food, it should also remind us that we are sinners; for although man would have taken food, even if he had not sinned, yet he would not have had to endure the pain and death caused by hunger. Hence we are become slaves to food because by food man tried to shake off his subjection to God. (Christian Education Book II. chap. 2. No. 5.)

With labour and toil shalt thou eat thereof all the days of thy life . . . . In the sweat of thy face thou shall eat bread till thou return to the earth, out of which thou wast taken. (Genesis iii. 17, 19.)

18. ST. GABRIEL. Angels being active and purely spiritual beings, have, by their very constitution, a real feeling of excellence and superiority over men; and they received from God the opportunity of renouncing this feeling by worshipping the deified manhood of Christ. (Theodicy No. 834.)

When He bringeth in the first begotten into the world, He saith: And let all the Angels of God adore Him. (Hebrews i. 6.)

19. ST. JOSEPH. If St. Joseph held on earth the dignity, so to speak, of the head of the house, he did so only as representing the Divine Bridegroom, to whom he had fully yielded and consecrated his bride. (Letters 5071.)

And Joseph found favour in the sight of his master, and ministered to him. (Genesis xxxix. 4.)

20. Now-a-days Jesus Christ is, as it were, a stranger to most Christians. Even by good people He is looked upon more as God than as Man; hence they almost seem to be afraid of approaching Him. He is not spoken of as lovingly and as frequently as He should be. Some even have a repugnance to speak freely to one another, and to express openly those feelings of love which they bear Him in their hearts. (Christian Education Book III. chap. 3. No. 5.)

Whosoever shall confess Me before men, him shall the Son of Man also confess before the Angels of God. (St. Luke xii. 8.)

21. When in spring-time nature puts forth anew all its beauty, when it clothes the earth with verdure and the trees with foliage, when sparkling waters flow and birds sing merrily; we who are endowed with reason should consider that man also is invited by his Creator to renew himself, and to raise his voice in concert with the inanimate and irrational creation, to sing the praises of his Lord. (Christian Education Book III. chap. 2. No. 9.)

Winter is now past, and the rain is over and gone. The flowers have appeared in our land. . . . . Arise, my love, my beautiful one, and come. (Canticle of Canticles ii. 11, 12, 13.)

22. Venial sins do not deprive the soul

of the grace of God, nor do they take away or even diminish the habit of charity. It may even happen that of two souls one has more defects than the other and yet has a far greater habit of charity. (Letters 7574.)

For a just man shall fall seven times, and shall rise again. (Proverbs xxiv. 16.)

23. Oftentimes faith and grace are in our souls, without our knowing it; we must not confound them with the feeling of faith and grace. Nor can it be supposed that our spiritual condition will change from one state to another in a short time, and without some grave cause. (Letters 2673.)

Believe God, and He will recover thee; and direct thy way, and trust in Him. Ecclesiasticus ii. 6.)

24. Above all, keep your mind tranquil, and do not imagine it is an act of virtue to depreciate yourself unreasonably, much less to want to gain virtue by violence and with agitation. When a person becomes upset and gives himself up to sadness and tears, he often arouses temptations and makes them stronger. (Letters 7574.)

In your patience you shall possess your souls. (St. Luke xxi. 19.)

25. THE ANNUNCIATION. To pass the holy-day of our Lady's Annunciation worthily, we must first adore the Divine Word, made Man for our salvation, and thank Him for so great a benefit; secondly, we must congratulate our Lady on her high dignity of Mother of God; and thirdly, we should resolve to recite the Angelus daily with great devotion. (Catechism No. 714.)

The Word was made Flesh and dwelt amongst us. (St. John i. 14.)

26. Jesus Christ is the director of all men. The more we hearken to His words the wiser do we become. "My sheep," says He, "hear My voice." (Christian Education Book I. chap 3. No 1.)

I am the Way, and the Truth, and the Life. (St. John xiv. 6.)

27. I am wont in my letters to imitate Cato who always ended his orations in the senate with *Delenda est Carthago* (Carthage must be destroyed). Now, we ourselves are this Carthage. Let us try, my dear brother, to make ourselves little, day and night; then shall we be happy in spite of all that may happen to us independently of ourselves. (Letters 7199.)

Whosoever therefore shall humble himself as this little child, he is the greater in the kingdom of heaven. (St. Matthew xviii. 4.)

28. When we are humbled, let us humble ourselves still more, then we shall be exalted: this is the doctrine of Jesus Christ. (Letters 6404.)

The greater thou art, the more humble thyself in all things, and thou shalt find grace before God. (Ecclesiasticus iii. 20.)

29. In order to discover whether we are truly detached from ourselves, it is well to examine whether we are glad to hear others praised. In particular I would advise you, my dear daughters, to see by a diligent self-examination if you are pleased when you find that praises are bestowed on your sisters. To yield even to the least feeling of displeasure or envy on such occasions would be a very grave defect indeed. (Letters 6649.)

Charity envieth not, ... seeketh not her own, ... rejoiceth with the truth. (1 Corinthians xiii. 4, 5, 6.)

30. A propensity to judge others rashly is a most dangerous fault in souls. This judgement is passed in haste, without any outward expression perhaps, and ofttimes almost unconsciously; hence we are prone to act with pride and presumption in consequence thereof. I deem that man perfect who is wholly free from rash judgement, and in this matter it is our bounden duty to watch with the utmost care. (Conferences on Ecclesiastical Duties ix. 15.)

Judge not, that you may not be judged. For with what judgement you judge, you shall be judged. (St. Matthew vii. 1, 2.)

31. We are not obliged to disclose to others all that we know; on the contrary, we should oftentimes remain silent, when speaking would prove prejudicial either to ourselves or to others. A man seldom repents of having kept silence; he rather regrets having spoken. Perfect virtue requires us to be sparing in the use of words which are innocent in themselves, but withal superfluous and profitless. This cannot be attained without very great watchfulness and self-mastery. Nevertheless we should shun that habitual silence which goes hand in hand with sadness and which renders a man a burden to his fellows. (Compendium of Ethics No 448.)

In many words shall be found folly. (Ecclesiastes v. 2.)

APRIL

1. The Eternal Father allowed His Incarnate Son to undergo death, among other reasons, to manifest the excess of evil to which man, corrupted by the sin of Adam, and under the power of the devil, was led ; to show what was the development of such a fatal germ, and what was the fruit of such a tree. The profound wickedness of that germ and its diabolical malice would not otherwise have appeared so fully to the eyes of man. Being hidden, it would have been judged much more leniently than it deserved, had it not reached the point of committing deicide in the sight of all nations. (Introduction to St. John's Gospel p. 201.)

Behold this child is set for the fall and for the resurrection of many in Israel. . . . that out of many hearts thoughts may be revealed. (St. Luke ii. 34, 35.)

2. How consoling is the right we have of addressing as our Mother the Mother of God, who gave us our Redeemer, who tended Him, and followed Him to the cross! There, at the foot of the dying Saviour's Cross, we obtained the right to call Mary our Mother, a right sanctioned by the word of Jesus: "Behold thy Mother." Our adoption, therefore, is the fruit of the sorrows of our Divine Redeemer and model, and of those of Mary. (Letters 1013.)

Forget not the groanings of thy mother. (Ecclesiasticus vii. 29.)

3. Why was the life of our Lord upon earth so short? In accordance with the law of celerity it behoved the Man-God to fulfil His celestial mission in the shortest time possible. Not one day of so precious a life was to be spent more than was necessary, not a single instant; every moment of it was numbered. (Theodicy No. 908.)

He gave Him the number of His days and time, and gave him power over all things that are upon the earth. (Ecclesiasticus xvii. 3.)

4. Christ may be said to have died twice; first, by suffering the torment of the imagination or internal sense, in the garden of Gethsemane; secondly, by enduring the agony of the bodily sense on Calvary. So that in Christ, humanity suffered all that it was capable of suffering, even to the death of the two component parts of man's sensitive nature, namely of the imagination and of the bodily sense: and all this undeservedly, for He was perfectly innocent; nay, on account of His eminent sanctity, He was deserving of the very contrary. (Introduction to St. John's Gospel p. 203.)

No man taketh My life from Me: but I lay it down of Myself, and I have power to lay it down. (St. John x. 18.)

5. It would be a crying injustice for an innocent man to be put to a most atrocious death, had he not himself renounced his right, and voluntarily accepted it. But such great sufferings endured by Christ without a cause became in His hands a credit of infinite value, which the Father's justice was bound to acknowledge, since it is a canon of eternal justice that all undeserved suffering should be compensated by an equal amount of joy. Now, what recompense, what joy did Christ demand from His Father? The salvation of His brethren, the rest of mankind. (Theodicy No. 760.)

But He was wounded for our iniquities, He was bruised for our sins; the chastisement of our peace was upon Him, and by His bruises we are healed. .... He was offered because it was His own will. (Isaias liii. 5, 7.)

6. A few days ago, I was reading a beautiful passage in the life of Father Caraffa, the seventh General of the Society of Jesus. He used to say that he had to meditate on three letters, one black, another red, and the third white; by which he meant to say his own sins, the passion of our Saviour, and the glory of the blessed. It seems to me that all subjects of Christian meditation may be reduced to these three points. By the black letter we come to know ourselves, and are enabled to direct our attention to the purification of our souls; by the red we are moved to imitate Christ in the mortification of human nature in all its parts; but with the white we are enabled to overcome discourage-

ment and to bear the desolation of spirit which sorrow for sins and other sufferings are apt to cause us; imitating in this also Christ our Lord, "who having joy set before Him endured the cross." (Letters 629.)

Oh, how have I loved Thy law, O Lord! It is my meditation all the day. (Psalm cxviii. 97.)

7. All that Christ is about to undergo, and is already undergoing, whether internally or externally, He endures for my sins. I am the cause of His sufferings. He endures them for my salvation, "Who loved me and delivered Himself for me." (Spiritual Exercises p. 208.)

For God so loved the world as to give His only begotten Son (St. John iii. 16.)

8. Yes, my brethren, we sinners have put Christ to death. This is the injury we have done to the Man-God; this the debt we have contracted. Who can pay such a debt? No one: we are all too poor. Yet if we cry to Him for pity, if we cast ourselves at His Feet, His Heart will be touched and He will forgive us so great an injury, so immense a debt. Lo! He prays for us who have crucified Him; He pleads our cause with His Eternal Father, saying, "Father, forgive them, for they know not what they do." (Sermons p. 38.)

All we like sheep have gone astray, every one hath turned aside into his own way: and the Lord hath laid on Him the iniquity of us all. (Isaias liii. 6.)

9. Jesus Christ crucified did not suffer on Calvary as performing a private devotion, but as fulfilling the highest pastoral duty, that of giving His life for His sheep. He was there exercising the highest prerogative in the Church, that prerogative which unites in one and the same person the Priest and the Victim acceptable to the Father, the source of all the prerogatives and of the entire ministry of Holy Church. (Letters 548.)

For it was fitting that we should have such a high priest, holy, innocent, undefiled, separated from sinners, and made higher than the heavens. (Hebrews vii. 26.)

10. When Christ died upon the Cross, His Body remained separated from His

Soul, though still united to the Divinity His blessed Soul, likewise united to the Divinity, descended into Limbo to release therefrom the souls of the just. It then returned and reanimated His Body, and Christ, leaving the sepulchre, appeared to many, and we may piously believe that the first to see Him would be His holy Mother. (Spiritual Exercises p. 219.)

But now Christ is risen from the dead, the first-fruits of them that sleep. (1 Corinthians xv. 20.)

11. To celebrate Easter worthily, the Christian ought in the first place to exult with a holy joy, as well for the glory acquired by Christ on this day, as for the good that he himself derives from it; secondly, he ought to adore and love the Sacred Humanity of our risen Lord; thirdly, he ought, if possible, to receive the Body of Christ, with a desire of rising spiritually to a new life; and fourthly, he should reflect on his own future resurrection. (Catechism No. 727.)

This is the day which the Lord hath made: let us be glad and rejoice therein. (Psalm cxvii. 24.)

12. Our Saviour's resurrection is the firmest foundation of our religion, because by it our Lord proves beyond all doubt that He is truly God, and consequently that His doctrine, whereon our whole religion is based, is Divine. (Catechism No. 721.)

And if Christ be not risen again, then is our preaching vain, and your faith is also vain. (1 Corinthians xv. 14.)

13. "We shall be like to Him" in Heaven. Oh, truly inebriating hope! But if we have not hearts of stone, the hope, nay the certainty of being like unto Him even on earth, will not be less dear to us. This certainly will strew our path with flowers; it will give a charm to the most distasteful occupations, especially those performed for the love of God and our neighbour. (Letters 6544.)

We are now the sons of God, and it hath not yet appeared what we shall be. We know that when He shall appear, we shall be like to Him, because we shall see Him as He is. (1 St. John iii. 2.)

14. St. Paul attributes our justification to Christ's resurrection, for, though it was merited by the passion, yet it was effected and completed by the resurrection, whereby Christ acquired His dominion over us, and was enabled to carry out His loving Heart's designs in our regard. Had not Christ risen, He could not have communicated to us His own glorious life; therefore we should not have risen again, but should have remained under the condemnation of sin. (Introduction to St. John's Gospel, p. 213.)

Who was delivered up for our sins, and rose again for our justification. (Romans iv. 25.)

15. When we awake in the morning, we should call to mind our future resurrection, the fruit of our Lord's merits. Before Christ, sleep bore the resemblance of death; now, death ought to seem but sleep to us: hence our Lord speaking of the daughter of Jairus said: "The girl is not dead but sleepeth." (Christian Education Book II. chap. 2. No. 10.)

It is now the hour for us to rise from sleep. (Romans xiii. 11.)

16. Had it not been for the resurrection, we should have had no hope of a future life. Christians therefore would have been the most miserable of men, for their only hope would be in this present life, while yet they have renounced its pleasures and regard it rather as death than life. (Introduction to St. John's Gospel p. 215.)

If in this life only we have hope in Christ, we are of all men most miserable. (1 Corinthians xv. 19.)

17. One virtue can no more be opposed to another than one truth can contradict another truth. But the judicious blending of the virtues that regulate contrary faculties and affections is an art which those who aspire to perfection ought especially to study. For in those who are truly perfect these virtues always go hand in hand. We see the same thing in music. The contralto voice, for instance, seems opposed to the baritone or bass; yet a skilful composer can so combine them as to produce a most pleasing harmony. (Letters 6648.)

But above all these things have charity

which is the bond of perfection. (Colossians iii. 14.)

18. The baptismal promises are called by St. Augustine our *most solemn vows.* To the primitive Christians they were sacred barriers against sin. The breaking of them was regarded as the direst of misfortunes, for they considered that after baptism the fall was deeper, the rising again more difficult, and the debt of punishment heavier. For this reason the trials of catechumens were prolonged in order that the new Christians might be strengthened in virtue before they made their solemn profession of leading strictly Christian lives. (Christian Education Book III. chap. xix. No. 2.)

It is much better not to vow, than after a vow not to perform the thing promised. (Ecclesiastes v. 4.)

19. If in former times men could apply themselves to one virtue in particular, now-a-days they must exhibit proofs of every virtue and leave no weak points. Grace is engrafted on nature, making use of its progress to shine with new light, and it would seem that the present development of the human race tends to make virtue more complete and solid. (Letters 548.)

Patience hath a perfect work: that you may be perfect and entire, failing in nothing. (St. James i. 4.)

20. Souls that have a due appreciation of virtue are never satisfied with their progress in the way of perfection. Their advancement seems to them too slow, too faltering. And truly it is so, for who amongst frail mortals can avow that he has done his duty, that he has toiled as much as the beauty of virtue and the goodness of God deserve? (Letters 6534.)

Not as though I had already attained, or were already perfect: .... But one thing I do: forgetting the things that are behind, and stretching forth myself to those that are before, I press towards the mark, to the prize of the supernal vocation of God in Christ Jesus. (Philippians iii. 12, 13, 14.)

21. Let us not deceive ourselves.

Without prayer a man cannot withstand evil nor keep united to God. He who prays little does little good: he who prays much does a great deal. We are bound to do great things in virtue of our profession of a life devoted to charity. Hence we ought to pray much; and if we do not we fail in our duty. (Letters 6503.)

Let nothing hinder thee from praying always. (Ecclesiasticus xviii. 22.)

22. In one who professes the Christian religion all should be reduced to this one point; to desire to be more just than he is, and to pray for it without ceasing, without measure or limit, so that he may be made one with Jesus, even as Jesus is one with the Father. (Maxims of Christian Perfection i. 3.)

That they all may be one as Thou, Father, in Me, and I in Thee, that they also may be one in Us. (St. John xvii. 21.)

23. God and the good angels infuse into the soul a spirit of true joy, banishing from it all the sadness and perturbation, that the devil may have caused. He on the other hand with fair-seeming but fallacious arguments seeks to destroy whatever joy he finds in the soul. (Spiritual Exercises p. 62.)

Thou hast made known to me the ways of life, Thou shalt fill me with joy with Thy countenance; at Thy right hand are delights even to the end. (Psalm xv. 11.)

24. There is this difference between the natural and the supernatural life: the former, having reached its maturity, then decreases; whereas the spiritual life may develop even more and more till death. (Catechetical Instructions No. 30.)

The path of the just, as a shining light, goeth forwards and increaseth even to perfect day. (Proverbs iv. 18.)

25. According to Christian teaching many temporal blessings may be obtained by prayer without any need of a miracle. But this truth implies another, namely, that God, when determining in the beginning the order of the events which were to follow in succession, foresaw all the prayers and desires of the just, ... and, with this prevision, He so disposed things, that those prayers should be answered in the natural course of events—answered, that is to say, by His granting either the very blessing which was asked, or else a greater one; and always in such a manner that, whichever of the two was granted, it should be made to accord with the universal good. (Theodicy No. 256.)

All wisdom is from the Lord God, and hath been always with Him, and is before all time. (Ecclesiasticus i. 1.)

26. Have we an unbounded love of truth? This is one of the questions which very few put to themselves; or if they do so accidentally, they reflect but little upon it; it seems to them too general, too common, and they do not trouble to gauge its vital importance. (Conferences on Ecclesiastical Duties xviii. 4.)

In no wise speak against the truth, but be ashamed of the lie of thy ignorance. (Ecclesiasticus iv. 30.)

27. A truly spiritual man, he who appraises things by the standard of faith and loves what is really good, can never incline more to the active than to the contemplative life. He rather prefers the latter as the more secure, and fears the former by reason of the many temptations and perilous conflicts with which it is fraught. Such a life of disquietude and distraction withdraws the soul from that union with its Creator which forms its only true good. (Conferences on Ecclesiastical Duties xix. 3.)

But one thing is necessary. Mary hath chosen the best part. (Luke x. 42.)

28. By her public holy-days the Church recalls the most conspicuous tokens of Divine Goodness in her behalf, namely, those which gave her birth, or those which have since added to her lustre. Likewise in the lives of Christians, there are tokens of God's goodness peculiar to each soul, bringing with them either salvation or an increase of grace. Let us then imitate the Church by commemorating these personal benefits. The anniversary of our baptism should hold the first place. (Christian Education Book III. chap. xx. No. 2.)

These are the holy-days of the Lord, which you must celebrate in their seasons. (Leviticus xxiii. 4.)

29. There are two kinds of prudence, called in Scripture the prudence of the spirit and the prudence of the flesh. It is not enough then to be prudent, we must be prudent according to the spirit; prudent with that prudence which goes hand in hand with the simplicity of the dove, according to the teaching of our Lord: "Be ye prudent as serpents and simple as doves." This is true virtue. By the dove, which we may take as an emblem of the Holy Ghost, we mean Divine Love. Our prudence then must not only creep on the earth as the serpent, but soar heavenward on the wings of the dove. (Conferences on Ecclesiastical Duties xvi. 3.)

For the wisdom of the flesh is death, but the wisdom of the spirit is life and peace. (Romans viii. 6.)

30. By poverty and chastity we give up all those things which we call our own. By humility and obedience we give up ourselves. (Conferences on Ecclesiastical Duties ix. 1.)

If any man will come after Me, let him deny himself and take up his cross and follow Me. (St. Matthew xvi. 24.)

MAY

1. On the first day of every month the Hebrews held a certain high holy-day, known as the Neomenia or New Moon. Up and down the year we, instead, keep the several holy-days of our Blessed Lady, whom, for her beauty of soul, the Church likens to the moon. (Christian Education Book III. chap. xviii. No 6.)

Who is she that cometh forth as the morning rising, fair as the moon, bright as the sun? (Canticle of Canticles vi. 9.)

2. Devotion to our Blessed Lady has a wondrous power in calming a troubled mind: the mild light of this our star is a comfort in every danger. (Letters 510.)

She was to them for a covert by day, and or the light of stars by night. (Wisdom x. 17.)

3. FINDING OF THE HOLY CROSS. How precious is this wood of the Cross! May our Lord enable us to understand its inexhaustible wealth! Therein we shall find all wisdom, all perfection, all good, the fulness of joy and a joy which does not pass away. (Letters 708.)

God forbid that I should glory, save in the cross of our Lord Jesus Christ; by whom the world is crucified to me, and I to the world. (Galatians vi. 14.)

4. I place my trust, after God, in our amiable Mother and leader, Mary; and as you advise, I commend this business also to her and remain at peace. The whole Institute is her child: let us leave her to act a mother's part. In the mean time I can assure you that she daily bestows fresh graces and new consolations upon me. (Letters 4268.)

I am the mother of fair love and of fear and of knowledge and of holy hope. (Ecclesiasticus xxiv. 24.)

5. If Jesus cannot refuse Mary anything because she is His Mother, and if Mary cannot refuse us anything because we are her children, is it not evident that nothing we need will be wanting to us, and that through her we can obtain all things? (Conferences on Ecclesiastical Duties xx. 12.)

And the king said to her: My mother, ask; for I must not turn away thy face. (3 Kings ii. 20.)

6. Truly the union of Christ and St. John was an indescribably beautiful pattern of perfect friendship. They must have been as like in mind and heart as they possibly could be since Christ deemed John the most fitting among His disciples to take His place near His Mother. On the Cross Jesus commended the two, as mother and son, to each other. I cannot imagine a greater or more touching proof of filial piety towards a mother than to provide her in her bereavement with a son most like the one she has lost, nor can I conceive a more striking token of friendship than to leave as a mother to one's friend the person nearest to oneself. Thus, having to withdraw from His Mother, Christ left her in His friend, an image of Himself, and having to quit His friend, He bequeathed to him a picture of Himself in Mary. (History of Love pp. 243, 244.)

When Jesus therefore had seen His mother and the disciple standing, whom He loved, He saith to His mother: Woman behold thy son. After that, He saith to the disciple: Behold thy mother. (St. John xix. 26, 27.)

7. What better safeguard can we have than the protection of our Blessed Lady? . . . . . Is not the dear name of Mary balm for all our wounds? I wonder how often you have experienced the comfort of this name, the aid of her who is the Mother of all who have recourse to her; for at the mere thought of God's Mother and ours, calm returns to the soul and serenity to the mind. Gladness accompanies the mere mention of her name; by invoking it we renew our courage even in moments of greatest discouragement and fiercest conflict, and we put the enemies of our soul to flight He who trusts in Mary cannot perish. (Letters 1013.)

I will give glory to Thy name, for Thou hast been a helper and protector to me. (Ecclesiasticus li. 2.)

8. If this holy Virgin, this most highly-favoured Mother of our Lord, is on the one hand the noblest member of the Church she may also be called with perfect propriety its Mother, since the Church was born when our Lord Jesus Christ was born. Hence it is that the Church has that close resemblance to Mary which a daughter bears its mother. And truly the Church resembles Mary, being like her endowed with both virginity and motherhood. (Sermons p. 303.)

Thou shall honour thy mother all the days of her life. (Tobias iv. 3.)

9. As the Church gives birth to Christ in us, so Mary gives birth to us in Christ. These two dear Mothers vie with each other in training us up and guiding us in the way of salvation. Both one and the other provide us with the means to obtain it. Mary in heaven graciously inclines her ears to our prayers; the Church on earth teaches us how to pray worthily to this heavenly Queen and Mother. (Sermons p. 303.)

He that honoureth his mother is as one that layeth up a treasure. (Ecclesiasticus iii. 5.)

10. Mary is rightly called priestess because she offered the Immaculate Victim in sacrifice. She may also be called the mother of the priesthood of the New Law, for she is the Mother of Jesus in whom the priesthood originated; for our priesthood is a participation of the priesthood of Christ. (Conferences on Ecclesiastical Duties xx. 12.)

Blessed art thou, O daughter, by the Lord the most high God, above all women upon the earth! . . . . for that thou hast not spared thy life, by reason of the distress and tribulation of thy people, but hast prevented our ruin in the presence of our God. (Judith xiii. 23, 25.)

11. After Jesus Christ, our model and beloved teacher is Mary most holy. . . . . Rightly is she considered by the Church as the type of wisdom, for there is no higher wisdom than to live tranquilly in God and to rejoice in Him with full confidence in His mercy, rendering heartfelt praise and thanks for all the works of His providence. (Letters 1165.)

In me is all grace of the way and of the

truth; in me is all hope of life and of virtue. (Ecclesiasticus xxiv. 25.)

12. Truly Mary is full of grace! She belongs to both Testaments. As member of the Old she has the grace of maternity; as member of the New she has that of virginity. . . . The dignity and majesty of her exterior gifts render her honourable before men; the abundance and perfection of her interior gifts make her pleasing before God. Therefore is she truly blessed among women on account of the fruit of her womb, blessed above all women as possessing for herself and bringing forth for others the perennial source of all blessings. (Sermons p. 306.)
Hail, full of grace, the Lord is with thee. Blessed art thou among women. (St. Luke i. 28.)

13. The Christian ought to meditate on and imitate at all times the profound humility of the Blessed Virgin Mary, whom the Holy Scriptures describe as in a constant state of calm, peace and quietness. The life of her own choice was one of humility, retirement and silence, from which she was drawn forth only by the voice of God, or by feelings of charity towards her cousin St. Elizabeth. (Maxims of Christian Perfection v. 7.)

He hath regarded the humility of His handmaid. (St. Luke i. 48.)

14. According to human judgement, who would have thought that so little would be said in the Holy Scriptures of the most perfect of all human creatures? There is no mention of any work undertaken by her; yet her life, which the blind world would regard as one of continual inaction, was declared by God to be the most sublime, the most virtuous and the most magnanimous of all lives. (Maxims of Christian Perfection v. 7.)

The works of the Highest only are wonderful, and His works are glorious and secret and hidden. (Ecclesiasticus xi. 4.)

15. Notwithstanding sin and the infection spread from it throughout the whole human race, God reserved for Himself a Virgin, free from all defilement of original sin, from whose blood, without the intervention of man, was begotten a Man who should be at the same time God, the Man-God who was to bring plentiful redemption unto mankind, and in this way to overthrow and shame the devil. Such a creation of the Divine Power and Wisdom was in a manner demanded by the law of variety, which required that this form also of human excellence should be realized. (Theodicy No. 754.)

Behold a virgin shall conceive and bear a Son. (Isaias vii. 14.)

16. Our Blessed Lady is uplifted in glory above all other creatures, because she is the Mother of our Saviour Jesus Christ, and because she is the most humble, most holy, and most perfect of all creatures. (Catechism No. 762.)

He that humbleth himself shall be exalted. (St. Matthew xxiii. 12.)

17. When Mary heard Elizabeth extol so highly her faith and her happiness in being chosen Mother of God, she was filled with a deep feeling of humility and gratitude, and began straightway to refer to God all her glory and to attribute to

Him alone her exaltation. She did not pretend not to know, as false humility is sometimes wont to do, nor did she try to conceal the dignity which had been bestowed on her. On the contrary she showed herself to be fully conscious of possessing it, and openly acknowledged it, but only as the work of the Lord. "My soul," she said, "doth magnify the Lord." (The Magnificat Explained No. 3.)

Glory shall uphold the humble of spirit. (Proverbs xxix. 23.)

18. While Mary declared herself to exult in God her Saviour, she made no allusion to being His mother. This was the secret of her heart, that unutterable secret from which she derived so great a joy, a joy all her own, which no one else could understand, and which could be imparted to no one else. "My secret to myself, my secret to myself." (Isaias xxiv. 16.) Others could only remotely imagine her joy, and she left them to do so without a word. (The Magnificat Explained No 7.)

Discover not the secret to a stranger. (Proverbs xxv. 9.)

19. Mary professed her faith in the Divinity of Jesus Christ before any one else in the New Law. She did so long before Saint Peter, who, for having said, "Thou art Christ, the Son of the living God," was made the foundation of the Church. Even before Christ was born she acknowledged Him to be God, before He could announce Himself to the world by His preaching or confirm it by His miracles. Full well, then, did she merit the eulogy pronounced by her cousin, "Blessed art thou, because thou hast believed." (The Magnificat Explained No. 8.)

And my spirit hath rejoiced in God my Saviour. (St. Luke i. 47.)

20. That unknown Virgin, hidden away from the world in a mountain village, and hardly known to her own kindred, ... heard the voice of countless numbers in all ages proclaiming her glories and calling her blessed. The word *blessed* signifies all that is most auspicious, most happy, all that imports the greatest good to a creature. Blessedness is at once the effect and the reward of perfect holiness. It conveys a eulogy that befits evangelical virtue only, for it is only the charity of Christ that merits blessedness. (The Magnificat Explained No. 11.)

Her children rose up and called her blessed. (Proverbs xxxi. 28.)

21. Does not the word *blessed* in the Magnificat contain a prophecy that has been already literally fulfilled? Throughout the whole world, the faithful delight in calling Mary *The Blessed Virgin*, rather than by any other endearing title. We who live eighteen centuries after Mary uttered this prophecy can bear witness to its fulfilment. We ourselves concur in fulfilling it every day. (The Magnificat Explained No. 11.)

Behold from henceforth all generations shall call me blessed. (St. Luke i. 48.)

22. He who wrought such great things in Mary is almighty. By styling Him the Mighty One, she sets forth the feebleness of men, and aknowledges that God alone is powerful . . . . As she recognized no other power but that which she knew belonged to God, so she could recognize no other greatness than the Divine. In saying that "He who is mighty" had done great things in her, she implied that the things done were great in relation to God Himself . . . . And truly the Incarnation which was accomplished in Mary was the greatest of all the divine works, because it was greater than creation itself. (The Magnificat Explained No. 13.)

He that is mighty hath done great things in me. (St. Luke i. 49.)

23. When Mary said, "The mercy of God is from generation unto generation to them that fear Him," she meant that they who have that which is less—namely, the just fear which holds them back from sin —shall also, in due course, have that which is greater—namely, love. They who do what they can will afterwards have the grace to do what now they cannot. All men can in some way fear God, with a just though natural fear. God does not owe them anything, and yet, as Mary said, He will show them mercy. (The Magnificat Explained No. 16.)

His mercy is from generation unto

generation to them that fear Him. (St Luke i. 50.)

24. Mary, who stands between the Old and New Dispensations, the last representative of the Patriarchs and the first of our Saviour's disciples, intends to teach us that, as the mercy which the Lord showed to those who feared Him had continued till it reached her, so too, as if beginning from her anew, it should continue to the end of the world, aye, and be even greater in all future generations than it had been in the past. (The Magnificat Explained No. 17.)

Blessed be the Lord God of Israel because He hath visited and wrought the redemption of His people . . . . . That we may serve Him without fear, in holiness and justice before Him, all our days. (St. Luke i. 68, 74, 75.)

25. The Arm of God in the style of Holy Writ means the Son of God, because the Son springs from the Father as the arm from the body. Mary therefore magnified the Father to whom the power belongs, and glorified Him in the Son of whom she is the mother, that is, the instrument used by the Father for the accomplishment of the great things which He designed to do on earth for men. (The Magnificat Explained No. 19.)

He hath showed might in His arm, He hath scattered the proud in the conceit of their hearts. (St. Luke i. 51.)

26. In that memorable Sermon on the Mount with which our Lord seems to have opened His solemn and public preaching, He taught a doctrine wholly new and unheard of. He said that they whom human wisdom declares to be most wretched are blessed; "Blessed are the poor," "Blessed are the meek," etc. Now our Lady's declaration that God exalts the humble makes it clear that, long before her Divine Son had preached this doctrine to others, He had revealed it to His beloved Mother, had infused it into her heart, and, as it were, had yielded to her the honour of being the first to proclaim it on earth. How just and natural it was that the Son should thus honour His Mother in this, as He had honoured her in all besides, so that she might seem even in this to be like other mothers, who are wont to be instructed before their children reach the age of knowledge. (The Magnificat Explained No. 22.)

He hath put down the mighty from their seat, and hath exalted the humble. (St. Luke i. 52.)

27. In the *Magnificat* we have set before us a picture of the merciful dealings of Divine Providence with the sinful human race, and marvellous praise and thanks are also given to that God who, having chosen His humble and faithful handmaid before all women, and by His Spirit formed the Redeemer in her immaculate womb, had thus done great things, not only to Mary, but also through Mary, to all the offspring of Adam. If you ponder well these things, at least while reciting the Canticle, you cannot help being fired with love, gratitude and unbounded reverence for her who is Mother of our God, and likewise the most tender mother of us all. (The Magnificat Explained No. 25)

For she is an infinite treasure to men, which they that use become the friends of God. (Wisdom vii. 14.)

28. Jesus is God and God is in Mary, as Mary is in God. Let us be then with Mary in Jesus, and with Jesus in God, now and for all eternity. (Letters 1705.)

Whosoever shall confess that Jesus is the Son of God, God abideth in him, and he in God. (John iv. 15.)

29. Oh, how much reason have we to exclaim with Holy Church, "Holy Mary, Mother of God, pray for us sinners, now, and at the hour of our death!" This is a most efficacious prayer, one that cannot go unheard, for by addressing Mary as Mother of God, we remind her why she is mother of man, thereby proclaiming her glory not by empty words of praise, but by extolling these gifts wherewith God Himself has adorned her, gifts surpassing the rose in fragrance and beauty, and the most brilliant gems in lustre and value. (Sermons p. 307.)

He hath clothed me with the garments of salvation; and with the robe of justice He hath covered me, as a bridegroom decked with a crown, and as a bride adorned with her jewels. (Isaias xi. 10.)

30. The Christian ought to ask of the Holy Ghost the gift of *understanding*, by which he may thoroughly understand and comprehend the sublime truths of faith; the gift of *wisdom*, by which he may judge rightly of divine things; the gift of *knowledge*, by which he may judge rightly of human things, and the gift of *counsel*, by which he may direct himself, applying the truths he has learnt to all the actions of his life. (Maxims of Christian Perfection vi. 2.)

Thou shalt send forth Thy Spirit, and they shall be created; and Thou shalt renew the face of the earth. (Psalm ciii. 30.)

31. Night and day let us turn our thoughts to Mary, let us have recourse to her in our needs, let us often speak of her, recount her glories and spread devotion to her. Let Mary be in our hearts, before our minds, on our lips and before our eyes, so that we may imitate her by walking blamelessly in her august and spotless presence. Thus shall we win for ourselves an abundance of Mary's choicest graces, graces during life and at the hour of death, since, after she has watched over us during life's weary pilgrimage, she will graciously receive our souls at death, and lead us to find unending bliss in the Divine Word, her Son, who is in the bosom of the Eternal Father. (Conferences on Ecclesiastical Duties xx. 12.)

He that shall find me, shall find life, and shall have salvation from the Lord. (Proverbs viii. 35.)

JUNE

1. The Heart of Jesus alone is tranquil and peaceful, and he who dwells in that Heart shares its peace; neither can persecution nor trouble destroy it, because these do not reach the Heart of Jesus where the faithful disciple makes his home. (Letters 4732.)
And the peace of God, which surpasseth all understanding, keep your hearts and minds in Christ Jesus. (Philippians iv. 7.)

2. Meditate on the humility, meekness and loving tenderness of which the Heart of Jesus is so full, and conform your heart to His. If you find in yours anything contrary to the Heart of Jesus (whether it has entered freely or not), make war on it to the death. (Letters 5566.)
But the meek shall inherit the land, and shall delight in abundance of peace. (Psalm xxxvi. 11.)

3. How beautiful is the thought I have

so often heard you* express, that we should have a *great heart:* that our Lord is great: and that the Christian does an injury to his Lord by not appreciating His greatness! Truly, nothing is so vast as not to seem narrow to the heart of the true disciple. (Letters 451.)

May God be gracious to you. . . . And give you all a heart to worship Him, and to do His will with a great heart and a willing mind. May He open your heart in His law. (2 Machabees i. 2, 3, 4.)

4. If the devil sees that we are brave, he loses courage and leaves us after a few assaults. But if he finds us weak and cowardly, he has just what he wants, he will give us no rest, and if we do not hasten to drive away our fears, the victory is his. We must pray unceasingly with the Royal Psalmist to be saved "from pusillanimity of spirit and a storm." (Letters 1175.)

Be subject therefore to God, but resist the devil, and he will fly from you. (St James iv. 7.)

* The Ven. Marchesa di Canossa.

5. O unspeakable goodness of God! He takes offence at our being disheartened; He exacts from us a courage as great (if that were possible) as His goodness, an infinite courage. (Letters 688.)

Say to the faint-hearted: Take courage, and fear not: behold. . . . . God Himself will come and save you. (Isaias xxxv. 4.)

6. You must fight hard against these thoughts of diffidence which are evidently a snare of the devil. It behoves you continually to increase your confidence in Jesus Christ. By persevering confidence you will be victorious over all your foes, or rather the grace of Jesus Christ will triumph in you. (Letters 6083.)

Have confidence in the Lord with all thy heart. (Proverbs iii. 5.)

7. Man of himself, when separated from Christ, is dead in respect to the life of grace his ultimate end: but he may truly be said to live when united to Christ, from whom he will receive a communication of His own supernatural life. (Catechetical Instructions No. 25.)

Abide in Me. . . . As the branch cannot bear fruit of itself unless it abide in the vine, so neither can you unless you abide in Me. (St. John xv. 4.)

8. I advise you to cultivate in the first place the spirit of recollection and interior fervour. You must learn to pray in your heart, to converse unceasingly with God, and speak to our Lord heart to heart, to walk in His Divine Presence, to call upon Him, to thank Him, to deplore your sins and humble yourself. (Letters 4490.)

And let the thought of God be in thy mind, and all thy discourse on the commandments of the Highest. (Ecclesiasticus ix. 23.)

9. The Christian who wishes to be perfect will lead a life of retirement, of silence, and of continual occupation. (Maxims of Christian Perfection v. 9.)

Work your work before the time, and He will give you your reward in His time. (Ecclesiasticus li. 38.)

10. The Church carries the Blessed Sacrament in procession with such pomp on Corpus Christi, firstly, to celebrate the victory gained by faith over so many heretics who impugn this mystery; secondly, to atone in some manner for the great irreverences and injuries which our Lord suffers from wicked men in this Sacrament of Love; thirdly, to revive the faith of Christians in this Sacrament, and to increase their devotion towards it. (Catechism No 751.)

These are the feasts of the Lord, which you shall call most solemn and most holy, and shall offer on them oblations to the Lord. (Leviticus xxiii. 37.)

11. To conquer the devil and to confound him in all his stratagems, the Eternal Father decreed to give another tree of life to the regenerated world far surpassing the first. This second tree is Jesus Christ. The Eucharistic Food and the hidden life of Christ which is contained therein, are the fruits of this tree. (Introduction to St. John's Gospel p 244.)

To him that overcometh I will give to eat of the tree of life, which is in the paradise of my God. (Apocalypse ii. 7.)

12. The Church calls the Holy Eucharist when given to the dying the *Viaticum*, and she obliges them to receive it, when they can do so, in order that at the moment of death they may have within them that life eternal which is the germ of their souls' resurrection after death. This shows that it is not good to scruple too much about giving the Viaticum again to the sick person who survives for some time after its reception. This, too, is one reason among others which urges upon Christians the importance of frequent Communion, since this it is which keeps them, like the wise virgins, ever ready for the coming of the spouse, by continually giving to them that life which manifests itself at the hour of their death. (Introduction to St John's Gospel p. 256.)

He that eateth My Flesh and drinketh My Blood, hath everlasting life, and I will raise him up in the last day. (St. John vi. 55.)

13. When we approach Holy Communion can we regard ourselves in any other light than that of poor sinners unconditionally surrendering to God as prisoners in His hands? Saint Francis of Sales used to say that precisely because we are imperfect we ought to communicate often, in order that, by approaching this source of all perfection, we may rid ourselves of our imperfections little by little, and become partakers of the Divine Perfection. (Conferences on Ecclesiastical Duties xiii. 8.)

Except you eat the Flesh of the Son of Man, and drink His Blood, you shall not have life in you. (St. John vi. 54.)

14. He who has received Baptism, together with the grace which it confers, is already a living member of the Body of Christ, and consequently he is in Christ and Christ in him. The Holy Eucharist preserves this union and mutual indwelling, just as food preserves the life of him who already has life. This is what is meant by Christ's word "abideth" ("abideth in Me and I in him") which implies permanence and duration. Again, food makes good what the living body loses day by day, and the same effect is produced in the soul by the Holy Eucharist, which cancels the lesser sins into which man daily falls, and again renews life within him. Thirdly, as food helps man to grow up, so does the Holy Eucharist cause Christ to increase in the new and spiritual man. (Introduction to St. John's Gospel pp. 246, 247.)

He that eateth My Flesh, and drinketh My Blood, abideth in Me, and I in him. (St. John vi. 57.)

15. Each time a man presumes to receive the Eucharistic Bread, he receives Christ sacrificed, and calls to his aid the death of Christ. . . . He, therefore, who brings to the Holy Table a guilty and unworthy conscience betrays his Master like Judas, but more basely than by a kiss. He sells Him to his passions and calls for His death; he does not desire the saving sacrifice, but the blood of the just that cries to heaven for vengeance. He is guilty of the Body and Blood of our Saviour, and in this sacrilege we may say of our Lord what the children of Jacob said of their brother: "A wild beast hath devoured him." (Christian Education Book III. chap. ix. No. 11.)

He that eateth and drinketh unworthily, eateth and drinketh judgement to himself, not discerning the Body of the Lord. (1 Corinthians xi. 29.)

16. It is true that with our heart at least we may seek and find Jesus everywhere; but our Lord .... condescended to make His presence not only real but corporeal also. He was pleased to take unto Himself a Body that should be like our own, so that our dead bodies might be restored to life by contact with His living Body which can never again be subject to death. And there is a sense peculiar to Christians by which we await this new happiness eagerly and perceive it when it comes. This spiritual sense it is which makes it impossible for you not to desire to be in the Church before the Tabernacle. (Letters 816.)

How lovely are Thy tabernacles, O Lord of Hosts! My soul longeth and fainteth for the courts of the Lord. (Psalm lxxxiii. 2.)

17. Had Christ's Sacred Humanity remained always visibly present to men, there would have been no need of the sacramental system. The very sight of His most Holy Manhood, His words, the contact with His Divine Body were all so many sensible channels through which a superabundance of grace could pass from Him to men. The touch of His sacred hands proved efficacious not only in curing bodily infirmities, but also in purifying and healing the soul, thus giving health " to the whole man" (John vii. 23). His words were "spirit and life" (John vi. 64), and His discourse "cleansed" man from all stain of sin (John xv. 3). The sight of the Sacred Humanity of Christ had power to uplift the soul of the beholder to the knowledge and contemplation of the Divine Word (John xiv. 9), and through Him of the Eternal Father. Therefore was the Sacred Humanity of Christ that sensible medium which, acting upon man's senses, sufficed to redeem and sanctify him. (Supernatural Anthropology Vol. III. p. 173.)

And Jesus said: Somebody hath touched Me; or I know that virtue is gone out from Me. (St. Luke viii. 45.)

18. How beautiful, how useful it is, to think of Jesus always!—to see Him in all things as the Apostles did, not only realizing that He is God (which thought is rather calculated to terrify us), but considering Him as Man, as one of ourselves, having a body like ours, a man truly subject to all human infirmities, sin excepted; one who suffers and rejoices with us, sympathises with us, comforts us, cheers us on and helps us, corrects and warns us; one who, like a true friend, is ever in our company. Ah yes indeed! Devotion to Jesus has grown cold with too many. How I wish that all Christians should do their utmost to restore and rekindle it! (Christian Education Book III. chap. iii. Nos. 6 and 7.)

For we have not a High Priest who cannot have compassion on our infirmities, but one tempted in all things as we are, without sin. Let us go therefore with confidence to the throne of grace, that we may obtain mercy and find grace in seasonable aid. (Hebrews iv. 15, 16.)

19. Speak often to your pupils of this dear Master of ours, let the Name of Jesus ring in their ears, let them behold Him present in all their occupations and taking part in all their games. If you can get them to form this habit of imagining Jesus as their inseparable companion in every place, at every moment and in every action of their lives, they will have acquired the practice of God's presence, of Christian watchfulness, of unceasing prayer, and of constant recollection. (Christian Education Book III. chap. iii. No. 7.)

They that fear the Lord will prepare their hearts, and in His sight will sanctify their souls. (Ecclesiasticus ii. 20.)

20. All meditations on the Sacred Humanity of Christ, and all reflections which help us to understand more clearly its grandeur and attractiveness are good and should be highly prized; for in this consists eternal life, that we know the Father, the only living God, and Jesus Christ whom He has sent. (Letters 5470.)

Now this is eternal life: That they know Thee, the only true God, and Jesus Christ whom Thou hast sent. (St. John xvii. 3.)

21. When summer ripens the corn, and the heat of the sun brings all fruit to maturity and gives even to animals an increased vitality, let us think of ripening ourselves for that season when the

Heavenly Husbandman will reap us for His granary. (Christian Education Book III. chap ii. No. 9.)

There remaineth therefore a day of rest for the people of God . . . . Let us hasten therefore to enter into that rest. (Hebrews iv. 9, 11.)

22. Our Lord, who as God is Truth itself, as Man is the great and only teacher thereof, and is consequently the model and example of all teachers. Let us look at this Divine Model. There we find no affectation, nothing forced or artificial. His method of explanation is clear, brief, profound and earnest; it is clothed with those similes and figures of visible things which are familiar to all and truly necessary to the undeveloped. (Letters 2771.)

He was seen upon earth and conversed with men. (Baruch iii. 38.)

23. Although every virtue is beautiful, nevertheless chastity and humility are singularly so . . . . . . Chastity prevents man from lowering his own dignity; humility keeps him from exalting it unduly. In these two virtues, therefore, the beauty of morality chiefly consists. (Sermons p. 374, in note.)

O how beautiful is the chaste generation with glory, for the memory thereof is immortal, because it is known both with God and with men. (Wisdom iv. i.)

24. The tenor of this solitary life is certainly at first hard, because it is full of privations. However, we are not in this world to enjoy ourselves. He who seeks for rest and enjoyment in this life deceives himself and courts many a bitter disappointment, for it is not God's will that they be found here below. (Letters 798.)

Looking on Jesus, the author and finisher of faith, Who having joy set before Him endured the cross, despising the shame, and now sitteth on the right hand of the throne of God. (Hebrews xii. 2.)

25. It is true that there is a great difference between the state of a soul radiant with sensible affection, light and joy, and that of a soul weak and disconsolate, immersed in gloom and sadness. But what of that? It is the *will of God* that the soul should be in darkness: therefore it is a blessing beyond compare, as great as God Himself, since the will of God is God. (Letters 5786.)

Make not haste in the time of clouds. . . . . Believe God and He will recover thee: and direct thy way, and trust in Him. (Ecclesiasticus ii. 2, 6.)

26. In the Old Testament it was a common belief, that no man could see God and live ; for God is a fire. "The Lord thy God is a consuming fire, a jealous God" (Deuteronomy iv. 24). He is truly a fire that consumes sins and sinners, but He is also a purifying fire, enkindling and vivifying the just. Hence it is written : "I will be sanctified in them that approach to Me, ... Be holy because I am holy" (Leviticus x. 3, and xi. 44). He therefore who approaches this fire is either consumed or *divinized*. (Conferences on Ecclesiastical Duties xx. 3.)

Was not our heart burning within us, whilst He spoke in the way? (St. Luke xxiv. 32.)

27. Apostolic men are certainly few in number, very few, for only those can be called such who are in an eminent degree men of prayer, and full of zeal in preaching the word of God. "We will give ourselves continually to prayer, and to the ministry of the word." (Letters 6464.)

By whom we have received grace and apostleship for obedience to the faith in all nations for His Name. . . . . For God is my witness, ... that without ceasing I make a commemoration of you. (Romans i. 5, 9.)

23. Could not Jesus Christ send as many labourers as He chose into the harvest field? He could and yet He would not. He wished His disciples to obtain the call by prayer, so intent was He on impressing upon them the necessity of receiving a divine mission before preaching the Gospel. (Letters 4977.)

Pray ye therefore the Lord of the harvest, that He send forth labourers into His harvest. (St. Matthew ix. 38.)

29. SS. PETER AND PAUL. On the feast of SS. Peter and Paul the faithful ought in the first place to thank our Lord Jesus Christ for having left to His Church

upon earth a visible head in the person of Saint Peter and of his successors the Roman Pontiffs; secondly, they should pray God to humble the enemies of Holy Church; thirdly, they should excite within themselves a veneration and affection for the person of the reigning Pontiff, and pray for him with great fervour. (Catechism No. 759)

Thou art Peter, and upon this rock I will build My Church, and the gates of hell shall not prevail against it. (St. Matthew xvi. 18.)

30. Who does not know how virtue fares on this earth? It is ever persecuted, and the more rare and choice it is, so much the more is it persecuted. . . . . But, wonderful consolation of our holy religion! The bitter draught which the saints drink is presented to their lips by Christ in that same chalice whereof He Himself first drank so willingly even to the very dregs. (Sermons p. 355.)

My grace is sufficient for thee, for power is made perfect in infirmity. Gladly therefore will I glory in my infirmities, that the power of Christ may dwell in me. (2 Corinthians xii. 9.)

JULY

1. Everyone must be ready to become a victim for the sake of truth and justice. (Directory for the Master of Novices.)
Blessed are they that suffer persecution for justice' sake for theirs is the kingdom of heaven. (St. Matthew v. 10.)

2. VISITATION OF OUR LADY. Chosen above all women to give the Saviour, the God-Incarnate to the world, Mary first carried the source of all holiness as was fitting, to the home of Elizabeth which she sanctified. She sanctified the mother of him who was destined to be the precursor of our Redeemer; she sanctified the precursor himself, anointing him as it were before his birth and so made him worthy of his exalted mission. (The Magnificat Explained No. 1.)
Whence is this to me, that the mother of my Lord should come to me? For behold as soon as the voice of thy salutation

sounded in my ears, the infant in my womb leaped for joy. (St. Luke i. 43, 44.)

3. All external things, not dependent on your own will (whether they be good or bad in themselves) may be, and are means employed by Divine Providence in the work of your sanctification. (Letters 2835.)
And we know that to them that love God all things work together unto good. (Romans viii. 28.)

4. Outside yourself there is for you neither good nor evil; all your good consists in your own sanctification, and all your evil in losing some degree of holiness. (Letters 2835.)
Who is he that can hurt you, if you be zealous of good? (1 St. Peter iii. 13.)

5. Either the time has come, or in the present course of events it will soon do so, when not only a fervent Catholic, but even anyone who retains a natural love of justice, will feel compelled to withdraw from the crowd, and to wear a distinctive badge; he will feel the necessity of close alliance with Catholics whose goodness, proved by their virtuous lives, is beyond question; for unfortunately, even among Catholics there is cockle to be found among the wheat. (Letters 297.)

If we say that we have fellowship with Him, and walk in darkness, we lie, and do not the truth. But if we walk in the light, as He also is in the light, we have fellowship one with another, and the Blood of Jesus Christ His Son cleanseth us from all sin. (1 St. John i. 6, 7.)

6. This is my principle in regard to works of charity : not to undertake anything of my own accord, nor to refuse to do a good work through weakness or cowardice. (Letters 2884.)

And this commandment we have from God, that he, who loveth God, love also his brother. (1 St. John iv. 21.)

7. The Church contains within herself the great organizing principle of the human race. She is destined to bring together the scattered races, and to form thereof one well-ordered body. When all mankind, according to our Saviour's promises, shall have been brought into the one fold under one shepherd, then will the work of creation be completed, the children of Adam will have achieved their destiny, and the entire human family will form that happy city which was foretold by the prophet Zacharias: "And Jerusalem shall be called the City of Truth." (Philosophy of Right Vol. II. p. 287.)

I will bring them, and they shall dwell in the midst of Jerusalem; and they shall be my people, and I will be their God in truth and justice. (Zacharias viii. 8.)

3. Jesus is the ever-faithful Spouse of of His Church, and His immaculate bride, the Church, is ever faithful to her Jesus. Jesus forms the chaste delights of the Church, and the Church forms the chaste delights of Jesus. The Church has no other will than that of Jesus her Head and her Lord, to whom she is subject, and to whom she yields a ready obedience, and Jesus wills nothing but the greater good of His Church. He would have her to possess all virtue, all grace, all glory, so that it is impossible that there should be the least discord or disunion whatever between the will of Jesus and that of His

Holy Church. (Treatises on Marriage. Ediz. Roma. Forzani. 1902. pp. 327-328.)

Christ loved the Church, and delivered Himself up for it. . . . . That He might present it to Himself a glorious Church not having spot or wrinkle or any such thing, but that it should be holy and without blemish. (Ephesians v. 25, 27.)

9. Do all you can to make your pupil appreciate the dignity of belonging to the Church of Jesus Christ, that immense, that Divine society which deserves all our love and should be the subject of all our thoughts. Beautiful is human friendship, but far more beautiful the love of Holy Church. Domestic affections are praiseworthy, praiseworthy is the love of our birthplace, and of our native land. But the ties of kindred, home and country should only be so many means of promoting the glory of God's Church; to the Christian they are but of a part of a greater and more excellent society. (Letters 568.)

Go forth out of thy country and from thy kindred and out of thy father's house, and come into the land which I shall shew thee. (Genesis xii. 1.)

10. The public profession of one's Faith is a duty which springs from the excellence of the Truth of the Gospel, and from the command which Christ gave to all Christians. It springs from the right which God has of being known, honoured and glorified in every possible way, and before all creatures; from the duty which every man has of longing for the coming and the extension of Christ's Kingdom upon earth; from the merits of Christ the following of whom should be deemed man's greatest glory, and from that perfect friendship existing between Christ and the Christian which prompts the latter to give glory to his Friend. Lastly, it springs from that supernatural love for his neighbour which makes a Christian ardently desire that the Gospel may be promulgated in every way and that all men may embrace it. (Philosophy of Right Vol. I. p. 239, in note.)

With the heart we believe unto justice, but with the mouth confession is made unto salvation. (Romans x. 10.)

11. The sacrifice which God commanded Abraham to make of his son, and the law whereby He reserved for Himself all the first-born, were the chief means which God made use of to temper the overweening love of parents for their children in order that it might not exceed the bounds fixed by that primary love of God, to which all other affections ought to be subservient. The separation of Moses from his own family, the sacrifice of Jephte, and Jonathan's generous friendship are examples which were ever present to the Jewish people, and the design of which was to curb the excessive and too exclusive love of parents for their offspring. (Philosophy of Right Vol. I. p. 424, in note.)

He that loveth son or daughter more than Me is not worthy of Me. (St. Matthew x. 37.)

12. Without supernatural light it is impossible to appreciate the value of obedience, for the light of natural reason will, with its sophisms, wage incessant war against it unto its utter destruction. (Letters 2591.)

Obedience is better than sacrifices. (1 Kings xv. 22.)

13. Instead of adapting the result of his own reasonings, let each one take for his guide the sublime and simple rule of the Divine Will, in imitation of Christ, who in speaking of His work did not say that He acted through this or that motive, but always said that he acted for the accomplishment of the will of His heavenly Father, and in order that the Scriptures, which contained the expression of that will, might be fulfilled. (Letters 3354.)

Because I came down from heaven, not to do My own will, but the will of Him that sent Me. (St. John vi. 38.)

14. Should there be a second Solomon in the Institute, he would be a source of grief to me rather than of joy and consolation, if he were not at the same time obedient. Nothing is valued in the Institute but the virtue taught by Jesus Christ, and this true virtue is summed up in obedience and charity. (Letters 4708.)

The sons of wisdom are the church of the just, and their generation obedience and love. (Ecclesiasticus iii. 1.)

15. One drop of morality and religion

is, in my estimation, worth more than an ocean of human learning. (Letters 37.)

Let no man deceive himself: if any man among you seem to be wise in this world, let him become a fool that he may be wise. For the wisdom of this world is foolishness with God. (1 Corinthians iii. 18, 10.)

16. OUR LADY OF MOUNT CARMEL. I know well that if there is anything which the devil hates and seeks to frustrate it is a religious vocation, and I know, too, that we shall not be able to succeed without the assistance of our Blessed Lady and without incessant struggle. Hence it is only natural that I should be afraid of the devil's putting hindrances in your way and devising delays . . . . At the same time I trust that Mary will assist you, if you act with an upright and pure intention, without human motives. (Letters 1438.)

To think therefore upon her is perfect understanding, and he that watcheth for her shall quickly be secure. (Wisdom vi. 16.)

17. The last article of the second part of the *Summa* is a great favourite of mine.

St. Thomas there shows that it is not necessary to ask counsel in the choice of the religious state, for this counsel has already been given by our Blessed Lord. Although our Divine Master has not enforced it as a precept, yet it is certain that no one can do wrong in embracing the religious state, if he do so with the pure intention of seeking to become perfect and to follow Jesus Christ more closely. (Letters 5649.)

It is great glory to follow the Lord, for length of days shall be received from Him. (Ecclestiasticus xxiii. 38.)

18. As to the doctrine concerning vocation to the religious life, it is true that, in a general way, it is a question of counsel, not of precept; consequently there is no sin in not following the call, for sin always implies violation of a precept. . . . On the other hand, it is certain that he who does not obey the call to religious life when he might do so, deprives himself of an infinite good; and to forfeit spiritual good is a great privation to one who has the light of faith. Besides this, we know nothing of the obligations entailed on others by the internal communications of grace; for it is certain that in particular cases, God requires of some men what He does not require of all, and that which is not commonly speaking a *precept* may become so to the individual. (Letters 3132.)

If thou wilt enter into life, keep the commandments . . . If thou wilt be perfect, go, sell what thou hast, and give to the poor. . . . and come, follow Me. (St. Matthew xix. 17, 21.)

19. ST. VINCENT DE PAUL. It is undoubtedly a meritorious act to do good to even one person; but to open up a lasting fount of blessings to many, and especially of spiritual blessings, is an undertaking the merit of which God alone can estimate. (Letters 200.)

Give, and it shall be given to you; good measure and pressed down and shaken together and running over shall they give into your bosom. For with the same measure that you shall mete withal, it shall be measured to you again. (St. Luke vi. 38).

20. In no religious order, according to the doctrine of St. Thomas, is it maintained that the religious is perfect; for the religious state is a school of perfection, and consequently presupposes imperfection in those who frequent it. (Letters 3288.)

Not as though I had already attained, or were already perfect; but I follow after, if I may by any means apprehend, wherein I am also apprehended by Christ Jesus. (Philippians iii. 12.)

21. The necessity of committing ourselves entirely to God is brought home to us by Jesus Christ when He teaches us to pray that we be not led into temptation. Only God can preserve us from those occasions which are to be found even in religion, though much more in the world—occasions of danger to the strongest virtue. Hence we find Jesus Christ Himself saying: "He hath given His angels charge over thee, to keep thee in all thy ways." . . . We are travellers on this earth and we know not whither we are going, whether into places full of dangers and difficulties or into those that are easy and safe. (Letters 622.)

Decline not to the right hand nor to the left. . . . For the Lord knoweth the ways that are on the right hand: but those are perverse which are on the left hand. But He will make thy courses straight, He will bring forward thy ways in peace. (Proverbs iv. 27.)

22. If we know ourselves we shall have an unbounded kindness and indulgence towards others. (Letters 1548.)

If a man be overtaken in any fault, you who are spiritual instruct such a one in the spirit of meekness, considering thyself, lest thou also be tempted. (Galatians vi. 1.)

23. So great is the unworthiness I perceive in myself that I can scarcely comprehend it, much less find words to describe it. A proof to me of the truth of all this is the joy I experience in thinking thus; for joy comes only from the truth, and God does not allow it to arise from error. (Letters 1165.)

Gladly therefore will I glory in my infirmities, that the power of Christ may dwell in me. (2 Corinthians xii. 9.)

24. A religious should be disposed to lay aside his own opinion and embrace that of others, but his humility and contempt of self should always be accompanied by an unswerving love of truth in obedience and charity. (Letters 615.)

Not minding high things, but consenting to the humble. Be not wise in your own conceits. (Romans xii. 16.)

25. Charity requires great things, and therefore our Institute expects great things of us; and great things cannot be achieved without a great development of charitable activity. The world requires great things and displays great activity but not great charity: the Institute requires immense activity, but all in the charity of Christ. (Letters 4512.)

Let us not love in word nor in tongue but in deed and in truth (1 St. John iii. 18.)

26. God has allowed the religious orders to deviate more or less from their primitive spirit, in order that no flesh should glory in His sight. All societies of men are corruptible, save only the Church of Jesus Christ, in virtue of a special favour which He obtained from His Father with a "strong cry and with tears." Therefore the Church is the work of God and not of man; it alone is founded on the Divine Word which is the firmament of the spiritual universe, as it is written: "Heaven and earth shall pass away but My word shall not pass away." (Letters 675.)

For all flesh is as grass, and all the glory thereof as the flower of grass . . . . but the word of the Lord endureth for ever. (1 St. Peter i. 24, 25.)

27. Nearly all religious communities develop sooner or later what is known in the world as *esprit de corps*, but this should be considered, when it is found in religious houses, as a limitation that springs from pride, a complacency in the society, which re-acts, however, on the members. Hence is weakened that charity which seeks to unite all men in one body, whatever be their ties, particular societies or differences. (Letters 548.)

One body and one Spirit; as you are called in one hope of your calling. (Ephesians iv. 4.)

28. Let our trust be in God alone. The favour of men never gives me encouragement without at the same time alarming me. (Letters 697.)

Cursed be the man that trusteth in man. . . . Blessed be the man that trusteth in the Lord, and the Lord shall be his confidence. (Jeremias xvii. 5, 7.)

29. The charges brought against us, in so far as they are false, should not alarm us, but we must try to profit by them, in order to know ourselves better and to get rid of such defects as may be disclosed to us by the criticism of others. Those who have enemies would do well to read for their consolation Plutarch's treatise: *De capienda ex hostibus utilitat.* (How to draw profit from enemies). (Letters 4512.)

But with modesty and fear, having a good conscience, that whereas they speak evil of you, they may be ashamed who falsely accuse your good conversation in Christ. For it is better doing well (if such be the will of God) to suffer than doing ill. (1 St. Peter iii. 16.)

30. God forbid we should deny the

truth; but we should set forth that portion of the truth which will produce the greatest good. The truth is sometimes a bitter pill, but so are the medicines given by physicians . . . . Our Divine Master was no less humble and no less meek when He used the word *fox* to Herod, and *hypocrite* or *blind* to the Pharisees, than when He prayed for those who crucified Him. The end we have in view is always one, and that is *charity*, even towards our enemies themselves; but the *means* are many, and among them is that of sometimes saying *blind* to the blind and *fox* to the fox. (Letters 4329.)

Answer a fool according to his folly lest he imagine himself to be wise. (Proverbs xxvi. 5.)

31. St. Ignatius Loyola. I myself firmly believe that all the holy founders of the great religious orders were men inspired, to whom God showed, as He did to Moses, the model of the order which they were foreordained to establish. (Letters 548.)

Look and make it according to the pattern, that was shown thee in the mount. (Exodus xxv. 40.)

AUGUST.

1. Shall I accuse the present generation of not reading the Scriptures? I would rather accuse them of not doing so devoutly. They read them coldly as they would read an ordinary book, and as if to judge rather than to be judged by them. Read them constantly, and, in so doing, follow the advice given in that golden book, the Imitation of Christ. (Book I. chap. v.) You can have no better rule. (Christian Education Book I. chap. 2. No. 4.)

All scripture inspired of God is profitable to teach, to reprove, to correct, to instruct in justice. (2 Timothy iii. 16.)

2. The Scriptures are one continual lesson of humility; they teach it in all sorts of ways, by means of the statements made, by the style, by the very words. (Letters 821.)

What things soever were written, were written for our learning, that through patience and the comfort of the scriptures we might have hope. (Romans xv. 4.)

3. To act with a spirit of intelligence simply means to follow the dictates of right reason, without allowing ourselves to be moved or disturbed by any passion whatever. Now the highest and most universal of all reasons for acting is that of doing always and in all things the will of God. (Letters 6648.)

Seek not the things that are too high for thee, and search not into things above thy ability, but the things that God hath commanded thee, think on them always. (Ecclesiasticus iii. 22.)

4. Had the religious state no other advantage than that of enabling us to fight our spiritual battles, not as individual soldiers, but in a compact body, this consideration alone should have much weight with one who seeks the greater glory of God: for a greater association implies a greater power, whether for good or for evil. (Letters 5649.)

And the multitude of believers had but one heart and one soul . . . . and with great power did the apostles give testimony of the resurrection of Jesus Christ. (Acts iv. 32, 33.)

5. Simplicity lies in love, prudence in thought. Love is simple, intelligence is prudent. Love prays, intelligence watches. *Watch and pray:* there you see prudence and simplicity reconciled. Love is like the moaning dove; the active intelligence is like the serpent that never falls or strikes against any obstacle, because it uses its head to feel its way along over the inequalities of the road. (Letters 6477.)

I fear lest, as the serpent seduced Eve by his subtilty, so your minds should be corrupted, and fall from the simplicity that is in Christ. (2 Corinthians xi. 3.)

6. A continual secret working is going on in every soul either for good or for evil. He who does not attentively watch this interior working and gradual transformation may one day become aware of the fact that he is altogether different from what he was formerly. He may find himself in a miserable state of spiritual languor or even mortal sickness, without being able to account for this fatal issue. (Letters 7378.)

Be mindful therefore from whence thou

art fallen; and do penance, and do the first works. (Apocalypse ii. 5.)

7. To abandon ourselves wholly to Divine Providence: there is perhaps no maxim which helps us more than this to obtain the peace of heart and evenness of mind proper to the Christian life. (Maxims of Christian Perfection iv. 1.)

He will overshadow thee with His shoulders: and under His wings thou shalt trust. (Psalm xc. 4.)

8. In the spiritual combat, provided we persevere and pray and believe in God's help, the victory may indeed be more or less prompt or slow, but it is certain. (Letters 7574.)

The Lord is the protector of my life: of whom shall I be afraid? . . . . . If armies in camp should stand together against me, my heart shall not fear. (Psalm xxvi. 1, 3.)

9. A good heart is to be preferred to great talents. Men of unusual power of mind are distrusted even by the world and as a rule have many enemies, whilst the good are loved by all. (Letters 598.)

With all watchfulness keep thy heart; because life issueth out from it. (Proverbs iv. 23.)

10. The first effect of the new life which man receives by his union with Christ is a moral power whereby he despises his natural life, physical and intellectual, and feels himself superior even to the fear of death. (Introduction to St. John's Gospel p. 169.)

Though I should walk in the midst of the shadow of death, I will fear no evils, for Thou art with me. (Psalm xxii. 4.)

11. The constancy of the good never fails them; because in that spiritual good which is neither obtained nor lost by violence, they have an inexhaustible store of spiritual strength, which renders them contented and invincible in their meekness. (Theodicy No. 882.)

A man of understanding is faithful to the law of God, and the law is faithful to him. (Ecclesiasticus xxxiii. 3.)

12. Holy souls do not suffer temptations to pride and vain-glory when God visits their souls with extraordinary supernatural favours and communications of light and grace, for during such times the sense of Christ's presence is most vivid. They experience, on the contrary, a feeling of the deepest humility, and are irresistibly prompted to give all the glory to God, as we see from the writings of the saints, especially of St. Teresa. (Introduction to St. John's Gospel p. 159.)

He that glorieth, let him glory in the Lord. For not he who commendeth himself is approved, but he whom God commendeth. (2 Corinthians x. 17, 18.)

13. Love correction, and receive it with a grateful heart and serene countenance, being mindful of those words of our Divine Master, Jesus: "He that is of God, heareth the words of God." (Letters 4436.)

Open rebuke is better than hidden love. (Proverbs xxvii. 5.)

14. All Christianity is summed up in these solemn words *In Christ*, because they express the real mystical union of man with Christ, in which union and incorporation real Christianity consists. (Introduction to St. John's Gospel p. 179.)

For in Christ Jesus by the gospel I have begotten you. (1 Corinthians iv. 15.)

15. ASSUMPTION OF B. V. M. On the Feast of our Lady's Assumption we ought, in the first place, to congratulate her upon the glory and happiness which she enjoys in heaven; secondly, we ought to excite within ourselves a great confidence in her powerful patronage, resolving to invoke her aid at all times in our needs; thirdly, we should beg of her to save us by her intercession, that we may see her and praise her for all eternity as she deserves. (Catechism No. 763.)

In the midst of her own people she shall be exalted, and shall be admired in the holy assembly; and in the multitude of the elect, she shall have praise. (Ecclesiasticus xxiv. 3, 4.)

16. When a man, about to do or to say something good, feels tempted to vanity, he should not on that account refrain from doing or saying that which tends to the divine glory, but having raised his mind to God and purified his intention, let him say to the enemy with St. Bernard: "I did not begin for you, neither will I leave off for you." (Manual of Spiritual Exercises p. 66.)

Take heed that you do not your justice before men, to be seen by them: otherwise you shall not have a reward of your Father Who is in heaven. (St. Matthew vi. 1.)

17. All Christians should remember to walk constantly in the Divine Presence. This exercise is sufficient to guard those who practise it faithfully from all sin, and indeed even to make them saints. (Catechetical Instructions 7.)

Blessed is the man that shall continue in wisdom, and that shall meditate in his justice, and in his mind shall think of the all-seeing eye of God. (Ecclesiasticus xiv. 22.)

18. Humility is a most lovable virtue. Everybody loves and wishes well to the humble man because he never gives offence, and willingly yields to the desires and feelings of others, even at the sacrifice of self.

He is readily listened to, and his words like some sweet balm penetrate the heart. (Conferences on Ecclesiastical Duties ix. 9.)

Where humility is, there also is wisdom. (Proverbs xi. 2.)

19. Let us ever start from this truth, that God is the God of Holiness and Holy is His Name. Sanctity is the perfection of His nature, the end of all His works; all that He does, all that He wills, is directed to this end. God therefore essentially wills His own sanctity, and the sanctity of His creatures. (Conferences on Ecclesiastical Duties xix. 7.)

This is the will of God, your sanctification. (1 Thessalonians iv. 3.)

20. ST. BERNARD. The very smallest degree of holiness acquired by man is of infinite value, and we may well give all to purchase so precious a gem and the field wherein it is hidden. I take this field to signify the religious state, in which, according to those beautiful words of St. Bernard: "Man lives more purely, feels more rarely, rises more speedily, walks more cautiously, receives the dew of grace more frequently rests more securely, dies more confidently ; his soul is cleansed more quickly and rewarded more abundantly." (Letters 5649.)

The kingdom of heaven is like unto a treasure hidden in a field, which a man having found, hid it, and for joy thereof goeth and selleth all that he hath, and buyeth that field. (St. Matthew xiii. 44.)

21. Try to be as kind and cheerful as possible in conversation, for a man who can maintain his soul in holy cheerfulness is less subject to temptations of envy or motions of anger. To this end, take dear St. Francis of Sales as your model. (Letters 2669.)

A glad heart maketh a cheerful countenance, but by grief of mind the spirit is cast down. (Proverbs xv. 13.)

22. A Christian should have the reasons of his own nothingness deeply engraved upon his mind ; firstly, those which prove the nothingness of all creatures ; secondly, those which humble mankind especially ; and thirdly, those which humble him personally. (Maxims of Christian Perfection v. 3.)

What is man that Thou art mindful of him, or the son of man that Thou visitest him? (Psalm viii. 5.)

23. Be generous with our Lord; do not fear to give too much, but desire and try to give Him more every day. Think whether you have anything that might be pleasing to Him, and then make the sacrifice of it. (Letters 2076.)

I do always the things that please Him. (St. John viii. 29.)

24. Of praise, commonly speaking, I take little account, because I know too well that it is not always sincere. But advice and admonitions, and even reproofs from friends, these are never deceptive; they bear the stamp of sincerity; they are gifts from the heart. (Letters 2884.)

Better are the wounds of a friend, than the deceitful kisses of an enemy. (Proverbs xxvii. 6.)

25. It is a mistake to suppose that we can instil humility into people by depressing and humbling them. No; it is rather by praising them in the Lord that we make them advance, and by humbling ourselves sincerely, without any affectation, and by actions rather than by words. (Letters 2778.)

Let nothing be done through contention, neither by vain-glory; but in humility let each esteem others better than themselves. (Philippians ii. 3.)

26. I advise you not to be too harsh with yourself, but to humble yourself continually with great gentleness and sweetness. Be persuaded of your own nothingness, and then you will not be surprised at the assaults of your passions. (Letters 2777.)

Son, when thou comest to the service of God. . . . prepare thy soul for temptation. Humble thy heart and endure. (Ecclesiasticus ii. 1, 2.)

27. St. Joseph Calasanctius. You are indeed privileged, destined as you are to lead to God many of the little ones so dear to our Lord. If the crime of scandalizing one of these children is denounced by Christ in such terrible words, surely there must be proportionate merit and ground of hope in caring for them and teaching them. (Letters 571.)

He that shall receive one such little child in My name receiveth Me. But he that shall scandalize one of these little ones that believe in Me, it were better for him that a mill-stone should be hanged about his neck, and that he should be drowned in the depth of the sea. (St. Matthew xviii. 5, 6.)

28. ST. AUGUSTINE. St. Augustine reprehends three classes of persons for their ignorance: firstly, those who imagine they know, and yet do not know; secondly, those who are conscious of their ignorance, but do not seek after knowledge in the right way; thirdly, those who are conscious of their ignorance, yet will not seek knowledge at all. (Treatise on Moral Conscience p. 256.)

Desiring to be teachers of the law, understanding neither the things they say nor whereof they affirm. (1 Timothy i. 7.)

29. Christ, loving all men, and rendering all men lovable in Him, has made them all neighbours. Thus the commandment of the law of Moses has received a new meaning, for it is no less true of the old law than of the new, that man is *bound to love his neighbour*. However there is this difference; under the old dispensation the love of one's neighbour had not strength enough to extend itself beyond the nation, whereas in the new law love receives from the grace of Christ and the work of redemption wings strong enough to bear it throughout the whole world. (Sermons p. 123.)

Thou hast redeemed us to God in Thy Blood, out of every tribe and tongue and people and nation, and hast made us to our God a kingdom and priests, and we shall reign on the earth. (Apocalypse v. 9, 10.)

30. One of the most favourable dispositions for advancing in perfection is to lay great stress even on small failings. When the soul is convinced that every defect in the moral order is a great evil, greater than any physical evil, it never thinks itself too severely punished or sufficiently humbled for its faults. This feeling, as noble as it is true, has always been conspicuous in the saints. (Letters 5337.)

He that contemneth small things shall fall by little and little. (Ecclesiasticus xix. 1.)

31. Prudence is acquired with age: the young do not see how profound and cautious a thing prudence is, and they easily imagine themselves to be gifted with it. The old man can see farther than the youth; therefore have great respect for age. You may hold it for a safe rule that prudence consists rather in refraining from action than in acting, and that we seldom are sorry that we did not speak or act, but often that we did. (Letters 2571.)

Stand in the multitude of ancients that are wise, and join thyself from thy heart to their wisdom, that thou mayest hear every discourse of God. (Ecclesiasticus vi. 35.)

SEPTEMBER

1. It is an undoubted fact that no religious who sincerely and constantly loves his vocation can ever perish. It is equally true that no religious who is lovingly attached to his vocation can go on living a tepid life for any length of time. The love of our vocation and serious defects are incompatible. Either we must rid ourselves of these faults, or we shall lose our vocation, for these two things are opposed to each other. (Letters 7387.)

Wherefore, brethren, labour the more that by good works you may make sure your calling and election. (2 St. Peter i. 10.)

2. Obedience though entire is never blind. It is blind in that it is not guided by human reasons, but it is not blind with respect to Divine reasons: it renounces mean and paltry considerations, but never loses sight of those which are great, universal, supernatural. By obeying, we may sometimes fail as regards some secondary object, but we cannot possibly be disappointed of reaching our final and absolute end, that which alone is true and gives value to other things. (Letters 5850.)

For it is not necessary for thee to see with thy eyes those things that are hid. ... For many things are shown thee above the understanding of men. (Ecclesiasticus iii. 23, 25.)

3. Humility, which is a Christian virtue intrinsically good and perfect, begets a lowly esteem of self and a proportionately high esteem of others. It persuades us to yield to others' opinions, though they be contrary to our own, and hence it leads us to obedience, in which there is always contained an act of humility—obedience to all men, as St. Francis of Sales says, but much more to lawful superiors. (Letters 5850.)

Be ye subject therefore to every human creature for God's sake. (1 St. Peter ii. 13.)

4. We must learn to remain united in

spirit with those we love: in spirit the most distant hearts can meet. The senses, indeed, crave for sensible intercourse, but we must mortify the senses with holy disdain. (Letters 5469.)

Behold how good and how pleasant it is for brethen to dwell together in unity. (Psalm cxxxii. 1.)

5. If the Superior occasionally makes mistakes, there is no error on the part of God, who permits a mistake only in so far as it will turn to the advantage of him who obeys. For the rest, God enlightens Superiors, bestowing on them the gift of wisdom precisely in that measure which is needful for obtaining the maximum of good for the obedient—that is to say, the highest degree of sanctity, and corresponding thereto an equally high degree of glory. Hence the Holy Spirit says emphatically: "An obedient man shall speak of victory." (Letters 5850.)

Obey your prelates and be subject to them, for they watch as being to render an account of your souls. (Hebrews xiii. 17.)

6. The perfection of the Gospel consists

in *self-denial:* "If any man will come after Me, let him deny himself." It is generally speaking only in the religious life, where obedience and indifference are in full force, that the real denial of self can be effectively and perfectly practised: for then every step we take is directed not by our own will but by obedience, that is to say, by God's will made known to us in the surest manner. (Letters 4188.)

For you are dead, and your life is hid with Christ in God. (Colossians iii. 3.)

7. Substantially, the Apostles were true religious and made perpetual vows, for they bound themselves perpetually and irrevocably to the following of Christ. It is the perpetual and irrevocable sacrifice of self that forms the excellence of the religious vows, and this unreserved sacrifice is not made by the faithful in general. (Letters 4188.)

Behold we have left all things, and have followed Thee. (St. Matthew xix. 27.)

8. NATIVITY OF OUR LADY. On our Lady's birthday, we ought firstly to congratulate her upon the singular privilege of being born holy; secondly, to call to mind with grief and confusion that we were born in sin; thirdly, to beg that she would assist us by her powerful intercession on this day to begin a new life, that is, a life of holiness and justice. (Catechism No. 766.)

I came out of the mouth of the Most High, the first-born before all creatures. (Ecclesiasticus xxiv. 5.)

9. I can never understand why people complain of not knowing how to employ their time; as if our Lord Jesus Christ, when He commanded us to love one another, had not opened to us a vast field, wherein to exercise and even to consume the strength and time of every one of us. This labour, assigned to us by our Divine Master, besides being more than sufficient, is also most noble and delightful. (Letters 7232.)

I must work the works of Him that sent me, whilst it is day: the night cometh when no man can work. (St. John ix. 4.)

10. Charity does not consist merely in feeding the hungry and clothing the naked;

it is equally an act of charity to avoid giving offence to any one. (Christian Education Book III. chap. xxii. No. 3.)
Charity is patient, is kind. (1 Corinthians xiii. 4.)

11. The charity that urges and presses us must not only be stronger than all our other affections, but it must render us superior to all sufferings. (Sermons p. 189.)
Love is strong as death. (Canticle of Canticles viii. 6.)

12. An excellent way of controlling the imagination is to write in large letters the names of Jesus and Mary, and to keep them before your eyes and read them over and over again with humble love and confidence. (Letters 6083.)
Put me as a seal upon thy heart, as a seal upon thy arm. (Canticle of Canticles viii. 6.)

13. Our love of one another is born of God. Eden was its native soil; innocence, its twin sister. (History of Love Book I. chap. i. No. 1.)

And every one that loveth is born of God. (1 St. John iv. 7.)

14. EXALTATION OF THE HOLY CROSS. Jesus Christ died for us: He has preserved us in life so far that we might be cleansed in His Blood. Our penance need not be long if only it is loving; and the best of all penances is patience under the crosses which He sends and adapts to our shoulders and helps us to bear. (Letters 4585.)

Christ also suffered for us, leaving you an example that you should follow His steps. (1 St. Peter ii. 21.)

15. We are sure of doing God's will whenever we fulfil the duties and obligations of our state of life, and try to do whatever is of obligation as perfectly as we can. (Conferences on Ecclesiastical Duties xix. 8.)

Not every one that saith to Me, Lord Lord, shall enter into the kingdom of heaven, but he that doth the will of My Father who is in heaven, he shall enter into the kingdom of heaven. (St. Matthew vii. 21.)

16. The Catholic Faith is holy; it has formed heroes of sanctity. These heroes, who were perfect examples of the most sublime virtue such as the world cannot know, not only adhered to the Catholic Faith, but it was from it alone that they derived the lights and the strength which made them what they were, models of innocence and generosity, who counted it as nothing to give their lives for the sake of Divine Love. (Letters 4807.)

This is the victory which overcometh the world, our faith. (1 St. John v. 4.)

17. We must be firmly persuaded that the mortification of our self-love is our greatest good. It is absolutely necessary that this great principle, containing the very essence of the Gospel, should not merely touch us on the surface, but should penetrate into the very depths of our heart. We must leave no stone unturned to obtain this disposition; we must pray, meditate, humble ourselves, entreat our superiors and above all conjure them to probe us to the quick. Here is salvation, to desire that this quick should be made dead by being stung and wounded. (Letters 4445.)

Unhappy man that I am, who shall deliver me from the body of this death? The grace of God by Jesus Christ our Lord. (Romans vii. 24, 25.)

18. There is no better way of overcoming our faults than to place ourselves when corrected on the side of him who gives the reproof, and then, by concentrating our attention on those faults, to endeavour to see them in all their deformity. God will then give us the grace (and what a grace it is!) to see our faults and to correct them. (Letters 1476.)

How good is it when thou art reproved to show repentance! for so thou shalt escape wilful sin. (Ecclesiasticus xx. 4.)

19. Beware of the imagination, and do not attend to its vain and restless judgements, but proceed in everything with intelligence, mindful of the teaching of our Divine Master: "I am come a light into the world, that whosoever believeth in Me may not remain in darkness." (Letters 4436.)

For all you are the children of light and children of the day; we are not of the night nor of darkness. (1 Thessalonians v. 5.)

20.* Let us be in no hurry to make our Institute *renowned;* no, for Heaven's sake! If notoriety come to us, let it not be of our seeking; let us trust in God and serve Him with great humility and peace, lest the spirit of the world enter into our works. Let us be on our guard against worldly maxims; "beware of men." (Letters 5326)

The kingdom of God cometh not with observation. . . . . For lo, the kingdom of God is within you. (St. Luke xvii. 20, 21.)

21. At the coming of autumn, the season of fruits and harvests, let us stir up holy desires after our end; let us sigh for that heavenly resting-place where we shall be for ever preserved from all danger of stain or corruption. (Christian Education Book III. chap. ii. No. 9.)

---

* On this day, in 1839, the Sovereign Pontiff, Gregory XVI, by Apostolic Letters, *In sublimi militantis Ecclesiæ solio,* approved the Institute of Charity. Hence the allusion. [Ed.]

But I am straitened between two, having a desire to be dissolved and to be with Christ, a thing by far the better. (Philippians i. 23.)

22. "Take no thought for the morrow." This simple act of banishing the thought of the future, with the fears that accompany it, is a great act of virtue and of self-abandonment into the loving hands of our Lord; it constitutes that walking in simplicity before God which is so highly commended in Holy Scripture. (Letters 4585.)

Be not therefore solicitous for to-morrow, for the morrow will be solicitous for itself. Sufficient for the day is the evil thereof. (St. Matthew vi. 34.)

23. Pilgrims as we are on earth, what can we do better than keep ourselves ever in readiness with the foot already uplifted, as it were, to go to any part of the world, whithersoever our Divine Spouse calls us? All the world is home to the servant of God, whose true home is heaven. (Letters 6112.)

For we are sojourners before Thee, and strangers. . . . . Our days upon earth are as a shadow and there is no stay. (1 Paralipomenon xxix. 15.)

24. The religious who cannot adapt himself readily to a change of superiors is certainly not mortified. All that he does, however austere, is no proof of genuine mortification, which must always be rooted in docility and pliableness of will; in short, in the renunciation of self. (Letters 2120.)
And be ye humbled under the mighty hand of God, that He may exalt you in the time of visitation; casting all your care upon Him, for He hath care of you. (1 St. Peter v. 6, 7.)

25. Every man, on the one hand, is always *useful*, and, on the other, is always *useless* for the designs of God. He is always *useful*, because God makes use of every man, good or bad, as a means for the glory of His kingdom, and for the good of other men. He is always *useless*, because the very best man that can be found, neither knows how, nor has the power, to do anything of himself for the glory of God's kingdom, or for the true good of other men, unless God Himself inspires and guides him. (Spiritual Exercises p. 156.)

Blessed be the Lord the God of Israel, who alone doth wonderful things. (Psalm lxxi. 18.)

26. Readiness to undertake all good works indifferently is the mark of perfection, and implies that universal love of one's neighbour which is the genuine charity of Christ. When in this disposition we are sure of pleasing our Lord and of doing His will rather than our own. Charity knows no repugnances; it loves all good and nothing but good. Self-love feels many repugnances and is therefore limited, for it does not love what is really good but only that which is so in appearance. (Conferences on Ecclesiastical Duties xix. 9.)

But I most gladly will spend and be spent myself for your souls. (2 Corinthians xii. 15.)

27. The Christian loves not change. In whatever condition he is placed, however lowly and abject it may be, and destitute of all that men care for, he is content and joyful; and he has no thought of change unless he knows it to be the will of God. (Maxims of Christian Perfection iv. 16.)

Let every man abide in the same calling in which he was called. (1 Corinthians vii. 20.)

28. We are always content. Our Society in whatever condition it may be is always complete and perfect in itself and seeks nothing further. All our desires should turn to our daily advancement in virtue; whether we be many or few matters little. The end of the Institute is the sanctification of its individual members; this is attainable under all circumstances, consequently the Society is always content and complete. (Letters 1349.)

Rejoice in the Lord always . . . . Be nothing solicitous. (Philippians iv. 4, 6.)

29. ST. MICHAEL.- The rebel angels were forthwith changed into demons, and we may well believe that, in conformity with the law of variety, as many of them fell as there were degrees of evil of which the angelic nature is capable, and that there remained faithful as many as are the degrees of goodness to which their nature can attain. (Theodicy No. 748.)

And that great dragon was cast out, that old serpent who is called the devil and satan, who seduceth the whole world, and he was cast unto the earth, and his angels were thrown down with him. (Apocalypse xii. 9.)

30. I must confess that I know by my own experience how easy it is, when you try to prove a thing very clearly to others, to use certain expressions that render the evidence too poignant, without exactly exaggerating. In a scientific treatise such expressions, when they do not exceed the truth, are natural and sound well enough, but in conversation they seldom produce a good effect. It is easy to give offence involuntarily in conversation; for people, as a rule, are offended when they see the evidence on our side is very strong or when we are very positive. (Letters 4512.)

He that setteth bounds to his words is knowing and wise. (Proverbs xvii. 27.)

OCTOBER

1. God created the angels for the same end for which He created man; that they might know, love, and obey God their Creator, and by this means become partakers of His nature, His sanctity and His bliss. (Catechism No. 57.)

Bless the Lord, all ye His hosts, you ministers of His that do His will. (Psalm cii. 21.)

2. If God permits evil spirits, within certain limits prescribed by His wisdom, to awaken in the human mind thoughts and designs which tempt or lead to evil, and commits it to His angels to suggest to the human mind thoughts which invite them to good or which direct their good undertaking to a happy end, He does not thus make direct use of His power. (Theodicy No. 870.)

Behold I will send My Angel, who shall go before thee, and keep thee in thy journey, ... Take notice of him, and hear his voice, and do not think him one to be contemned. (Exodus xxiii. 20, 21.)

3. In many passages of the Gospel God is likened to the father of wild and lawless children whom he afterwards reclaims. It is not said, however, that on that account these disobedient and rebellious children cease to be His children. This we see especially in the parable of the Prodigal Son, who properly represents a dissipated Christian wandering from his father's home. Yet the father acknowledges him for his son as soon as he returns, because the son has the features and marks whereby he can be recognized as a son, albeit in tatters, covered with noisome filth and pale and gaunt with hunger. Similarly, no matter how much the baptized Christian has set at defiance his Heavenly Father, he does not thereby forfeit the condition of son which was given to him by the impress of the baptismal character, and the Church still claims him as her subject and child. (Supernatural Anthropology Vol. III. p. 283.)

And now, O Lord, Thou art our Father, and we are clay : and Thou art our Maker, and we are the works of Thy hands. Be not very angry, O Lord, and remember no longer our iniquity: behold, see we are all Thy people. (Isaias lxiv. 8, 9.)

4. Bear in mind the saying of the enlightened St. Francis of Assisi: "We know just as much as we practise." (Letters 4457.)

Be ye doers of the word and not hearers only, deceiving your own selves. (St. James i. 22.)

5. A man who is united to Christ does not care to become possessed of the few and short-lived goods of this life, either by inheritance or by labour and cunning. He knows that he possesses all things in Christ, and that all things are at his disposal whenever he needs them for the attainment of his own supernatural end, which alone he values as his true good. Hence he feels the blessedness of that poverty proclaimed by Christ, to which the kingdom of heaven is promised. (Introduction to St. John's Gospel p. 172.)

As needy, yet enriching many; as having

nothing, and possessing all things. (2 Corinthians vi. 10.)

6. Saying and doing are two very different things, and the devil does not sleep during the interval which elapses between them. Christ will not sleep either, if only we will watch with Him; yet our very watching is His own gift to us. (Letters 1208.)

Watch ye, and pray that you enter not into temptation. (St. Mark xiv. 38.)

7. The great art of Divine Providence in purifying and perfecting us consists in placing us in circumstances entirely opposed to our will; in this way we are obliged to mortify and master this will, and to keep ever on the watch. If everything were to our liking, we should go to sleep, and never know what it is to fight valiantly. (Letters 1228.)

But this every one is sure of that worshippeth Thee, that his life, if it be under trial, shall be crowned; and if it be under tribulation, it shall be delivered; and if it be under correction, it shall be allowed to come to Thy mercy. (Tobias iii. 21.)

8. The Apostle teaches that our natural life as children of Adam would not be so corrupt, nor wage so fierce a war against the spirit of Christ, were it not urged on by the angels of darkness, who acquired a sway over human nature and the material world when our first parents ate of the forbidden fruit. (Introduction to St. John's Gospel p. 184.)

Put you on the armour of God, that you may be able to stand against the deceits of the devil. (Ephesians vi. 11.)

9. It is hard to say whether we should more ridicule or deplore the unreasonableness of men who vent their spleen against secondary causes, such as persons and things, regarding these as the authors of their misfortunes. . . . In reality, the sun, clouds, wind, fire, earth, animals, even men themselves, do neither more nor less than God commands or permits them to do. Persons and things are only means which God employs as He pleases for the accomplishment of His ends. (Catechetical Instructions No. 11.)

Who is ignorant that the hand of the

Lord hath made all these things, in whose hand is the soul of every living thing, and the spirit of all flesh of man? (Job xii. 9, 10.)

10. Many Doctors of the Church affirm that all our spiritual profit is derived from meditation. Grace is obtained by meditation only, by interior prayer; for vocal prayer is of itself useless unless it be accompanied by some act of the mind. (Conferences on Ecclesiastical Duties iii. 3.)

I will pray with the spirit, I will pray also with the understanding. (1 Corinthians xiv. 15.)

11. To meditation we must add some spiritual reading either of the Holy Scriptures or of other pious books; and this reading may serve also as a preparation for our meditation. Then again there is the examination of conscience, and this too is a kind of meditation on ourselves; and when it is made with impartial justice and a sincere wish to advance in the way of God, it is of immense advantage to a Christian. (Conferences on Ecclesiastical Duties iii. 5.)

Attend unto reading . . . . Meditate upon

these things . . . . that thy profiting may be manifest to all. Take heed to thyself. (1 Timothy iv. 13, 15, 16.)

12. Nothing tends so much to rekindle the fire of charity in the heart as friendly conversation about the things of God when it is sincere and simple. Unfortunately, speaking of God and of our Lord Jesus Christ is the last thing Christians think of, although God should be the dearest and most familiar object of their thoughts and conversations. Some indeed go so far as to say that politeness requires the exclusion of religious topics from conversation, nay, that profound respect for God forbids us to talk of Him. A strange kind of respect that which banishes God from Christian society! (Sermons p. 115.)

Be thou an example of the faithful, in word, in conversation, in charity, in faith, in chastity. (1 Timothy iv. 12.)

13. The Christian must not in the least be disheartened, nor stop in his course, if external things make an impression on him; but let him with inward recollection renew without ceasing his desire of justice alone, until he feels no voluntary desire for anything on this earth, either great or small, except with reference to justice, that is, to do the thing most pleasing to God. (Maxims of Christian Perfection i. 7.)

Take heed to thyself, and attend diligently to what thou hearest, for thou walkest in danger of thy ruin . . . . Love God all thy life, and call upon Him for thy salvation. (Ecclesiasticus xiii. 16, 18.)

14. The more man tries to purify himself from wilful faults, the more light does he receive to discover his hidden faults, and thus he is enabled to rid himself of these also. Saint Teresa compares the supernatural light which enters a soul to a sunbeam shining into a room through the windows, and showing the numberless specks of dust that crowd and jostle in the air where previously nothing at all was visible. In like manner the enlightened soul perceives many defects in itself where formerly it saw none. (Treatise on Moral Conscience p. 262.)

Ye that fear the Lord, love Him and

your hearts shall be enlightened. (Ecclesiasticus ii. 10.)

15. ST. TERESA. Saint Teresa desired that all her doubts, perplexities and spiritual combats (and hers were many and very great), should be examined by the light of solid theological doctrine, not by the imagination. You ought to desire the same. (Letters 7574.)

Hold the form of sound words, which thou hast heard of me in faith. (2 Timothy i. 13.)

16. Humility is a generous virtue. It makes a rational submission of the whole man, but especially of his reason, to Him whom Holy Scripture calls the only Wise. It recognizes and confesses the limits that have been fixed to the human mind, and thus it prepares the way for faith, and through faith leads man direct to truth ; while pride darkens his mind, and is a prolific source of errors. No matter how absurd may be the errors in which the proud man becomes entangled, he feels quite satisfied so long as he can flatter himself with a high opinion of his own worth, and thus hide from himself his weakness and imperfection. (Theodicy No. 166.)

Humiliation followeth the proud and glory shall uphold the humble of spirit. (Proverbs xxix. 23.)

17. It is far better to love, contemplate, and pray with the least possible reflection on ourselves, on what takes place in our souls, or on what we are doing. Our good is in God and in our neighbour, not in self. What we have to do is to think of God rather than of ourselves, to seek Him especially in our neighbour, and not perplex ourselves by counting the steps we take in our search for Him. (Letters 5164.)

It is good for me to adhere to my God, to put my hope in the Lord God. (Psalm lxxii. 28.)

18. In order that you may attain the desirable steadfastness in well-doing, accustom yourself to consider good in itself and to love it for its own sake. Then nothing will have power to divert you from your good resolutions, since good is always good, be its surroundings what they may. (Letters 5546.)

Seek ye good and not evil, that you may live; and the Lord the God of hosts will be with you. (Amos v. 14.)

19. The principle of fulfilling the duties of the state in which God has placed the Christian, and of spending all his time well, will make him love labour, and in a particular manner the art or occupation that he professes, to which he should apply with diligence. (Maxims of Christian Perfection vi. 6.)

And I have found that nothing is better than for a man to rejoice in his work, and that this is his portion. (Ecclesiastes iii. 22.)

20. Heavenly doctrine is of such a nature, that even were a man capable of reducing it to a theory and expressing it in words, yet his pupils would not understand it, unless God Himself opened their minds to His light; or else they would misunderstand it if He did not direct their attention to the truth. (Letters 6477.)

Understand what I say, for the Lord will give thee in all things understanding. (2 Timothy ii. 7.)

21. Try to become proficient in whatever you are taught; but, if any sister who has done what she could does not succeed as well as she would like, let her be resigned without disquieting herself, and let her still go on with all diligence, labour and constancy, omitting nothing on her part that would ensure success, being mindful of what the Divine Master said to the servant who had hidden the one talent under ground: "Wicked and slothful servant . . . . thou oughtest to have committed my money to the bankers, and at my coming I should have received my own with usury." (Letters 4436.)

Labour as a good soldier of Christ Jesus. (2 Timothy ii. 3.)

22. To be fastidious in the choice of books—never satisfied with any, always desirous of having more in the hope of finding better ideas in new works, or in those we have heard of—but do not possess, betrays levity of mind and a formed bad habit. It shows that we neither appreciate nor thoroughly understand the books we actually do read, and that we do not see the extent and the practical application of the maxims they teach. (Christian Education Book I. chap. i. No. 1.)

But continue thou in those things which thou hast learned, and which have been committed to thee, knowing of whom thou hast learned them. (2 Timothy iii. 14.)

23. When we are able to see without displeasure that others differ from us in matters of opinion, we show, not only that there is charity in our hearts, but that we love the truth itself; for he who loves truth knows full well and acknowledges that he is fallible, and that others may see the truth in a clearer light than he does. (Conferences on Ecclesiastical Duties xviii. 5.)

But avoid foolish questions and genealogies and contentions and strivings about the law, for they are unprofitable and vain. (Titus iii. 9.)

24. ST. RAPHAEL. The flight into Egypt, and the return of the Holy Family, their journey to Bethlehem, the travels of our Blessed Lord, of St. Paul and the other apostles, the journeys of young Tobias and of the Israelites in the desert, and such like, are suitable subjects for meditation when travelling. (MS. Rules for Religious when travelling.)

May you have a good journey, and God be with you in your way, and His Angel accompany you. (Tobias v. 21.)

25. In the greatest misfortunes which befall us, there is always the hand of infinite love. "God is Love." If the designs of His mercy concealed under the rigour of His justice were disclosed to us, if they were unveiled to our eyes as they are to the gaze of the heavenly intelligences, we should know no other feeling whether in prosperity or in adversity but gratitude and joy (Letters 6189.)

My son, neglect not the discipline of the Lord, neither be thou wearied whilst thou art rebuked by Him. For whom the Lord loveth He chastiseth (Hebrews xii. 5, 6.)

26. We do well to be quite sure of this, that there is a precept binding us to seek after moral truth—in other words, after the knowledge of our own duties—and that this must be done in the right way. It was in atonement for breaches of this precept that sacrifices for sins of ignorance were offered in the Old Law. Hence that terrible saying of St. Paul: " If any man know not, he shall not be known." (Treatise on Moral Conscience p. 257.)

In all thy works let the true word go before thee, and steady counsel before every action. (Ecclesiasticus xxxvii. 20.)

27. Against nothing did Jesus Christ inveigh more strongly than against the false consciences of the Pharisees. For since this is the most hidden of sins and the source of innumerable others, our Saviour had to use great force, almost violence, to uproot it and to bring to light its hidden canker. (Treatise on Moral Conscience p. 182.)

There is a way which seemeth just to a man, but the ends thereof lead to death. (Proverbs xiv. 12.)

28. The Catholic religion alone has real enemies. Other religions only differ from each other as one lie differs from another; whereas the Catholic religion differs from all as truth does from falsehood. She, therefore, has enemies essentially; others only accidentally. (Apologetics p. 105.)

Remember My word that I said to you. The servant is not greater than his Master. If they have persecuted Me, they will also persecute you. (St. John xv. 20.)

29. Man is naturally active, and he likes to exert his activity externally. Grace alone draws him to the interior, from the visible to the invisible, from the body to the spirit. Grace detaches man from creatures and unites him to his Creator. Since then this is the peculiar work of grace, which acts in quite the reverse way to nature, it is not surprising that it is a more perfect work, for grace is more perfect in its movements than nature. Neither is it surprising that our Lord praised Mary's life in preference to Martha's, eulogising it in those memorable words: " Mary hath chosen the best part, which shall not be taken from her." (Conferences on Ecclesiastical Duties xix. 3.)

All the glory of the king's daughter is within. (Psalm xliv. 14.)

30. All that is said by spiritual writers who treat of prayer, concerning divine operations in the interior of the soul, may be most profitably studied by those whose duty it is to direct others: but it is of little avail—nay, it may be dangerous for souls and a cause of anxiety and intellectual difficulty for them—if they wish to apply these teachings to themselves. (Letters 5164.)

But above all these things pray to the Most High that He may direct thy way in truth. (Ecclesiasticus xxxvii 19.)

31. The Saints are made one body with Christ and are called His co-heirs He Himself is the heir, because He died under the appearance of fallen man and rose again as the new man, and thus inherited, not only whatever belonged to the old man, but all other things besides. In like manner also, since the faithful are members of His very Body, so they too are invited to share with Him in this royal and magnificent heritage. (Introduction to St. John's Gospel p. 172.)

For the Spirit himself giveth testimony to our spirit, that we are the sons of God. And if sons, heirs also, heirs indeed of God and joint heirs with Christ. (Romans viii. 16, 17.)

NOVEMBER

1. ALL SAINTS. On the feast of All Saints, the faithful should conform to the Church's intentions in the institution of this festival. They should, first, honour with due devotion all the Saints in Heaven; secondly, invoke their patronage; and thirdly, yearn for the moment when they will be united with them in Heaven. (Catechism No. 773.)

Behold the tabernacle of God with men, and He will dwell with them, and they shall be His people, and God Himself with them shall be their God. And God shall wipe away all tears from their eyes: and death shall be no more, nor mourning, nor crying, nor sorrow shall be any more, for the former things are passed away. (Apocalypse xxi. 3, 4.)

2. ALL SOULS. We can alleviate the pains of the souls in Purgatory, and hasten their admission into Heaven by our prayers, alms-deeds, and all manner of good works, especially by the Holy Mass and the Indulgences of the Church. (Catechism No. 771.)

It is a holy and wholesome thought to pray for the dead, that they may be loosed from sins. (2 Machabees xii. 46.)

3. As the Christian should ever bear in mind the glory of Heaven, so also, in all his actions, he should remember that all things else decay, that they pass away quickly, and that death is the means of reaching his last rest in Heaven. (Maxims of Christian Perfection ii. 8.)

And they that use this world, as if they used it not; for the fashion of this world passeth away. (1 Corinthians vii. 31.)

4. I have always held it for certain that God, who in His paternal goodness has lavished so many benefits on us during life, will not fail to do so in a special manner at the hour of death, first, by decreeing the kind of death and those accompanying circumstances which may be most conducive to our eternal welfare, and, secondly, by bestowing on us abundant graces. He acts like a father who is more anxious to provide for the welfare of his children at those times when he knows that they have greater need of his fatherly care. (Letters 5057.)

But the souls of the just are in the hand of God, and the torment of death shall not touch them. (Wisdom iii. 1.)

5. The hope that our dear departed ones have already received the reward of their good works, or at least that their salvation is for ever secured, is such as to forbid us to bewail their loss. Although withdrawn from our mortal gaze, they are not dead, but are living a more perfect, an immortal life. (Letters 5143.)

In the sight of the unwise they seemed to die, and their departure was taken for misery, and their going away from us for utter destruction; but they are in peace. (Wisdom iii. 2, 3.)

6. She who has lost by death the dearest object of her affections has all the more right to call God her Father, Protector, and Spouse. Being freed from human ties, she has acquired greater liberty to give herself to God and to devote herself to works of charity and piety. Hence St. Paul, speaking of the woman who has no husband, says: "She thinketh on the things of the Lord, that she may be holy both in body and spirit." (Letters 5320.)

Thou hast broken my bonds: I will sacrifiec to Thee the sacrifice of praise, and I will call upon the name of the Lord. (Psalm cxv. 16, 17.)

7. When a person of known virtue departs this life, though we may have full confidence that his salvation is secure, nevertheless we must not presume that poor human nature is fit to appear before the All-holy at once, without being purged from every defilement: consequently we must pray for this soul in case it should need our help. (Letters 5320.)

If any man's work abide, ... he shall receive a reward. .... If any man's work burn, he shall suffer loss: but he himself shall be saved, yet so as by fire. (1 Corinthians iii. 14, 15.)

8. In His immense goodness our Lord Jesus Christ has left us a most efficacious

means of hastening the purification of departed souls, and of making them by the application of His merits worthy to look upon His face. Besides being a proof of our faith in prayer, in suffrages, and in good works in behalf of the holy souls, this efficacious application of the merits of Christ is at the same time most precious to our dear departed, and most consoling to the survivors, who can thus hasten the moment of their admission into the joys of heaven. (Letters 5604.)

Blessed are they that wash their robes in the Blood of the Lamb, that they may have a right to the tree of life, and may enter in by the gates into the city. (Apocalypse xxii. 14.)

9. The simple knowledge that faith cannot deceive us because it is founded on God's word, is most consoling, for it assures us that our departed friends, who believed and hoped in Christ, are not really dead. They have acquired a better life than they had in this world ; so that they would not willingly return from their abode of peace to the troubles and dangers of this present life. This thought alone is surely more than enough to dry our tears and to change our sorrow into heavenly consolation. (Letters 5929.)

And we will not have you ignorant, brethren, concerning them that are asleep, that you be not sorrowful, even as others who have no hope. For if we believe that Jesus died and rose again, even so them who have slept through Jesus will God bring with Him. (1 Thessalonians iv. 12, 13.)

10. We should reflect that though the souls in Purgatory suffer, yet they do so willingly. Even were it in their power, they would not return again to this world. They are truly happy in hope, honoured by the angels and raised to the dignity of spouses of God. Their glorious destination is secure for ever. There only remains a brief delay of that happy moment when they shall see their Divine Spouse, and, all beautiful and resplendent with glory, shall be introduced by Him into His nuptial chamber. (Letters 4607.)

And though in the sight of men they suffered torments, their hope is full of immortality. (Wisdom iii. 4.)

11. How consoling is the doctrine of Purgatory! How many sins, which in the estimation of man seem mortal, will be judged by God to be but venial, either from want of knowledge of the evil or from want of deliberation; for God takes into account man's personal dispositions. (Letters 6189.)

Hear Thou from heaven, from Thy high dwelling-place, and forgive, and render to every one according to his ways, which Thou knowest him to have in his heart: (for Thou only knowest the hearts of the children of men). (2 Paralipomenon vi. 30.).

12. I verily believe that if, by a right estimate of this life of sense and of the flesh, we could detach ourselves from all affection to it—for at best it is but an incommodious and corruptible prison—and were able by the energy of our will to dwell in that other serene and spiritual form of existence assumed by the soul on its release from the shackles of the body, we should experience a spiritual joy at the thought of our own death and that of our friends, which would lessen, or rather overcome, the natural sadness caused by death. This joy springs not from man's own nature but from Christ our Lord, with whom we are united as members with their head, and who enjoys an immortal and glorious life. Our Lord gives a communication of this same life to His members here below, but more abundantly still when they pass from earth to heaven; where He fully supplies the loss they sustain by being deprived of their bodily senses. (Letters 6500.)

But we are confident, and have a good will to be absent rather from the body, and to be present with the Lord. (2 Corinthians v. 8.)

13. What is our whole life on earth but a novitiate for Paradise? (Letters 953.)

Do not therefore lose your confidence.... For patience is necessary for you, that doing the will of God you may receive the promise. For yet a little and a very little while, and He that is to come will come, and will not delay. (Hebrews x. 35, 36, 37.)

14. As disobedience usually springs from pride, so obedience is the natural effect of humility: and as every sin is an act of pride, according to St. Thomas, so is it likewise an act of disobedience. Contrariwise, as every meritorious and virtuous act springs from humility, so in like manner it springs from obedience. (Conferences on Ecclesiastical Duties x. 1.)

Pride is the beginning of all sin (Ecclesiasticus x. 15.)

15. Chastity, expressed by the girding of the loins—which St. Perer couples with sobriety, saying, "Therefore having the loins of your mind girt," etc.—has its seat in the purity and serenity of a mind free from everything carnal. Sobriety contributes much to the attainment of this state of mind which enables man to raise himself to the hope of that glorious grace offered to him, when Jesus Christ will manifest Himself at the hour of death, and again at the last day. (Introduction to St. John's Gospel p. 187.)

Wherefore having the loins of your mind girt up, being sober, trust perfectly in the grace which is offered you in the revelation of Jesus Christ. (1 St. Peter i. 13.)

16. One who is occupied in external works may be secretly actuated by the praise and good-will of his fellow-men, and he may easily take complacency in his own doings, especially if they are great and striking. The interior man, on the other hand, who works out his own sanctification in secret, has nothing in which he can take complacency; in fact, all his endeavours and his very profession itself tend to self-abasement and concealment: he loves to be unknown and accounted as nothing. (Conferences on Ecclesiastical Duties xix. 3.)

Look to yourselves, that you lose not the things which you have wrought, but that you may receive a full reward. (2 St. John i. 8.)

17. Everything is promised to the prayer of faith, notwithstanding the obstacles set by nature's laws. It seldom happens that one of the faithful seeks a miracle for his own benefit; he asks for these miracles that others may know the truth of the Gospel. He who already believes and is satisfied with the ordinary course of Divine Providence in which he rests, has no need of miracles: his only desire is to become a saint, for which end external miracles are not necessary. Hence, as he neither desires nor longs for them, he cannot possess that faith which obtains them. (Introduction to St. John's Gospel p. 170.)

Jesus answering saith to them: Have the faith of God. Amen I say to you, that whosoever shall say to this mountain, Be thou removed and be cast into the sea, and shall not stagger in his heart, but believe that whatsoever he saith shall be done, it shall be done unto him. (St. Mark xi. 22, 23.)

18. If there be one thing that we should wish to know with certainty, it is surely our eternal salvation. Yet God has not willed that even the Saints should be fully assured of their salvation so long as they are in this world. So completely is their state hidden from them, that not even St. Paul himself could say that he was justified. (Letters 5570.)

There are just men and wise men, and their works are in the hands of God; and yet man knoweth not whether he be worthy of love, or hatred. But all things are kept uncertain for the time to come. (Ecclesiastes ix. 1, 2.)

19. Let us not be like unbelievers who have no hope beyond this miserable life. Our best, our only good is in the next world. There is our haven, our country; there, our crown of justice and the triumph of mercy. (Letters 5929.)
Unto the hope of life everlasting, which God who lieth not hath promised before the times of the world. (Titus i. 2.)

20. The disciple of Jesus Christ should live constantly in an interior solitude, in which, all other things being, as it were, set aside, he finds God alone and his own soul. (Maxims of Christian Perfection v. 1.)
If you return and be quiet, you shall be saved: in silence and in hope shall your strength be. (Isaias xxx. 15.)

21. Presentation of Our Lady. Turn to Mary and say to her frequently: My dear Virgin Mother, drive the enemy from my soul. (Letters 2540.)

He that looketh upon her shall remain secure. (Ecclesiasticus iv. 16.)

22. St. Cecilia. David's gentle touch of the harp refreshed the troubled soul of Saul and so rejoiced him that the evil spirit departed from him ; and how like he is in this to our Divine Master Who moved men so sweetly and powerfully, and made the world resound with the accents of the new and heavenly harmony of His law of love ! For love, like blended chords of a sweet harp, penetrates the human heart, subdues it, banishes Satan, and establishes within it the reign of Christ. (History of Love Book II. chap. xvii, §. 1.)

Draw me, we will run after thee to the odour of thy ointments. (Canticle of Canticles i. 3.)

23. Each one performs his task as a workman in the great workshop of the same master ; and at the end of the day each one receives his wages, not according to the kind of work he has done, but according to the fidelity, the assiduity, the earnestness, and the love for his master, with which he has laboured. (Maxims of Christian Perfection vi. 7.)

Behold I come quickly, and My reward is with Me, to render to every man according to his works. (Apocalypse xxii. 12.)

24. Blessed are they who put a favourable construction on everything that can be so construed, and who regard the virtues and not the failings of their brethren, provided, however, that these brethren be not confided to their care. (Letters 6167.)

Charity thinketh no evil. (1 Corinthians xiii. 5.)

25. Every act and feeling of pride presupposes unbounded ignorance and consummate foolishness. (Conferences on Ecclesiastical Duties ix. 4.)

Every proud man is an abomination to the Lord. (Proverbs xvi. 5.)

26. When we shall have attained eternal bliss, as, by God's mercy, I trust we may, we shall see how deluded we were in dreading so much, both for ourselves and those dear to us, the passage from this miserable life to that of everlasting peace and joy. Let us seek one thing alone, to devote ourselves wholly to God whilst we have time. (Letters 1213.)

Behold how they are numbered among the children of God, and their lot is among the saints. Therefore we have erred from the way of truth. (Wisdom v. 5, 6.)

27. If there be any link whatsoever between human hearts which is not unlawful and condemned, the charity of Jesus Christ, far from destroying or weakening it, absorbs and ennobles it, giving to it the very form and nature of the charity of Christ. (History of Love, Book III. chap. xi. §. 1.)

Purifying your souls in the obedience of charity, with a brotherly love, from a sincere heart love one another earnestly. (1 St. Peter i. 22.)

28. We can and we ought to perform our spiritual duties even when overwhelmed by other cares. The time due to them is precious, and it is time well-spent, even for the very sake of our other occupations, which derive spirit and life from them. Guard jealously therefore this time of union with God, and make every effort in it, and be constant. (Letters 5489.)

Let nothing hinder thee from praying always. (Ecclesiasticus xviii. 22.)

29. In order to spend well the holy season of Advent, we must, first, abstain from sin, and purify our souls more and more by the Sacraments of Penance and the Holy Eucharist; secondly, we must ardently long for the coming of Jesus Christ into our souls, as did the Patriarchs who prayed so fervently that He might come on earth; thirdly, we should assist at the services of the Church during this time; fourthly, we must meditate upon the mystery of our Lord's Nativity, and stir up within ourselves feelings of gratitude and of tender devotion towards His Sacred Humanity; fifth, we must do works of penance. (Catechism No. 658.)

Prepare ye the way of the Lord, make straight His paths. (St. Luke iii. 4.)

30. The fact that a work is good and charitable does not entitle us to conclude that it would be conducive to our perfection; we must weigh all its circumstances. In the first place we must consider whether we are induced to undertake the work from human motives merely; next, whether it is calculated to disturb our union with God, to interfere with our other duties, or to injure the good works which we have already undertaken; whether it is above our strength, conformable to the will of superiors, and not prejudicial to our equals; in a word, whether the work, considered on all sides, is truly good in itself, calculated to edify our neighbours and to sanctify our own soul. (Conferences on Ecclesiastical Duties xix. 8.)

Send wisdom out of Thy holy heaven and from the throne of Thy Majesty, that she may be with me and labour with me, that I may know what is acceptable with Thee. (Wisdom ix. 10.)

DECEMBER

1. The first means of obtaining the spirit of prayer certainly is to pray, and to ask this grace from God most earnestly. (Conferences on Ecclesiastical Duties ii. 8.)
Lord teach us to pray. (St. Luke xi. 1.)

2. I consider it so important to say our vocal prayers with attention, that I venture to say, that if all who pray were to do so with actual attention to the meaning of the words, and with devotion of heart, the entire Church would be renovated and all the faithful reformed. (Conferences on Ecclesiastical Duties ii. 12.)
By all prayer and supplication praying at all times in the spirit. (Ephesians vi. 18.)

3. Keep before your eyes the example of the great Apostle St. Francis Xavier, who was ready to leave all the good he was doing at the first sign of his Superior's will. Indeed he would actually have done so, if he had not died before the command to leave his great mission in the East could reach him. So long as you do not place yourself in this state of indifference, so long as you do not work with such holy indifference and self-control as to be ready to relinquish the work in hand, believe that you have reason to be afraid of yourself, afraid that your work may not really be acceptable to God. What would it avail you to toil hard and do a great deal if on the Day of Judgement you found that you had done nothing really pleasing to God? (Letters 1642.)

What shall it profit a man if he gain the whole world and suffer the loss of his soul? (St. Mark viii. 36.)

4. We must understand that the power of our soul by which we directly communicate with God and are united with Him, is different from all those powers by which we act externally. It follows, then, that when a man has attained to a certain state of contemplation and union, he works with the faculties which regard external actions without at the same time being at all disturbed in that quiet and that repose in God which are enjoyed by the ruling power of his nature. . . . So desirable a state is reached only by those faithful and constant souls who in the beginning make great efforts to mortify themselves, and pray with intense fervour and assiduity. (Letters 6648.)

God is charity; and he that abideth in charity abideth in God, and God in him. (1 St. John iv. 16.)

5. St. Francis of Sales, the saint of sweetness and discretion, says that a soul can never uplift itself to God, unless the flesh is mortified and subdued. (Conferences on Ecclesiastical Duties viii. 7.)

But I chastise my body, and bring it into subjection. (1 Corinthians ix. 27.)

6. Jesus Christ wished that the precept of love, which He spoke not to our ears but to our hearts, should be the glorious and most precious badge of His disciples. (Letters 4890.)

By this shall all men know that you are my disciples, if you have love one for another. (St. John xiii. 35.)

7. If our instruction or our work stops at literature, or grammar, or philosophy, or any other branch of human knowledge, and does not reach the Gospel in which is salvation, it is as if we stopped half way on a journey, and never reached our destination. (Letters 6503.)

The root of wisdom is to fear the Lord. (Ecclesiasticus i. 25.)

8. THE IMMACULATE CONCEPTION OF B.V.M. To keep well the feast of our Lady's Immaculate Conception, the Christian ought firstly, to thank Almighty God for having sent the Mother of our Saviour into the world: secondly, to congratulate our Lady on her Immaculate Conception, and to render honour to this her unique privilege; and thirdly, to remember with humble confusion the original sin in which he himself was conceived. (Catechism No. 664.)

Thou art all fair, O my love, and there is not a spot in thee. (Canticle of Canticles iv. 7.)

9. We wrong God no less by distrust than by presumption. Pusillanimity is no less unbecoming to a Christian than temerity. Are we not happy in this, that we not only may have courage but are bound to have it, in all the circumstances of life? (Letters 688.)

Woe to them who are faint-hearted, who believe not God, and therefore they shall not be protected by Him. (Ecclesiasticus ii. 15.)

10. Oh, how much reason there is to fear and tremble for the young in this wicked age! When I think of the risks to which a young man is exposed in the world, I feel that God must work a prodigy whenever He conducts one safe and sound to the eternal city of the Saints. (Letters 6189.)

Remember thy Creator in the days of thy youth. (Ecclesiastes xii. 1.)

11. Our body and all our human nature is a heavy burden to carry. We have to drag it about like a cart. It reminds me of one of those carts described by Manzoni in his account of the plague at Milan, a cart-load of pestilential flesh. (Letters 911.)

For the corruptible body is a load upon the soul, and the earthly habitation presseth down the mind that museth upon many things. (Wisdom ix. 15.)

12. I hold that erroneous consciences which are slightly culpable, and the works that proceed from them, form the multitude of light and unnoticed faults into which the just themselves fall, according to the saying of Holy Scripture : " A just man shall fall seven times." Holy men greatly lament such faults, and labour hard to purify themselves from them. (Treatise on Moral Conscience p. 206.)

The heart is perverse above all things, and unsearchable ; who can know it ? (Jeremias xvii. 9.)

13. I feel sure that should a man, by God's singular favour, be able to avoid those sins which arise from a false conscience, he might be regarded as a sun without spot and as having reached the summit of perfection, for he could not commit sin without advertence and a clear reproach of conscience ; and in these circumstances sin can easily be avoided by every good and God-fearing person. (Treatise on Moral Conscience p. 207.)

Create a clean heart in me, O God, and renew a right spirit within me. (Psalm l. 12.)

14. Let us be firm, resting in God without hesitation or wavering—nothing wavering. Let us wait in faith—wait for the Lord,—for He has no better means of teaching men than by making them wait. The general defect of men is excessive haste. How wise a man is who knows how to wait! (Letters 962.)

The Lord is my portion, said my soul, therefore will I wait for Him . . . . It is good to wait with silence for the salvation of God. (Lamentations iii. 24, 26.)

15. Our Lord gives us a great lesson in the seventh chapter of St. Matthew's Gospel in which He shows us that, not only must we do *good*, but do it *well*, if we would gain merit and save our own souls. It is quite possible to save the souls of others and lose our own. (Letters 1642.)

Many will say to Me in that day: Lord, Lord, have we not prophesied in Thy name, and cast out devils in Thy name, and done many miracles in Thy name? And then will I profess unto them, I never knew you: depart from Me, you that work iniquity. (St. Matthew vii. 22, 23.)

16. There should not be too great a scarcity of conveniences (in our houses), but there must be no ornament. By conveniences I do not understand those things which help us to be indolent, but those which help us to be more active, for conveniences are of two kinds. (Letters 702.)

Give me neither beggary, nor riches: give me only the necessaries of life. (Proverbs xxx. 8.)

17. No one is necessary to the Divine Redeemer for glorifying His Church, that is, for redeeming mankind from the slavery of sin, in which all men are equally born. Only in His mercy, freely bestowed, does He choose from among the redeemed those whom He pleases to raise to such an honour, employing usually for His greatest works that which is weakest and most contemptible in the eyes of the world. (Maxims of Christian Perfection iii. 3.)

Neither doth any man take the honour to himself, but he that is called by God as Aaron was. (Hebrews v. 4.)

18. THE EXPECTATION OF OUR LADY. Far from supposing that Mary suffered at all in giving the Sun of Justice to the world, I hold .... that when the time of the Redeemer's birth was accomplished, she must have been filled with such untold and heavenly joy, and rapt in an ecstasy of love so sublime, that man cannot conceive it. This joy must have been to her a foretaste of the bliss of Heaven. (Letters 5071.)

Drop down dew, ye heavens, from above, and let the clouds rain the Just: let the earth be opened and bud forth a Saviour. (Isaias xlv 8.)

19. Solitude is dear to me, because by its means we can plunge into deep thought and create around us a better society than that of man. (Letters 812.)

Our conversation is in heaven. (Philippians iii. 20.)

20. The love of Jesus sanctifies the

natural affections, so directing them that they do not blind us, but rather help us to do all possible good to our neighbour. Human and natural affections, of themselves, do not discern what is good; but affections governed by the love of Jesus discern what is truly good, and make use of human things to render thanks for the attainment of that true good outside of which there is only the appearance of good. (Letters 688.)

But you are washed, but you are sanctified, but you are justified in the name of our Lord Jesus Christ, and the Spirit of our God. (1 Corinthians vi. 11.)

21. Winter invites us to reflect on the fleeting nature of all things human, the instability of all human appearances, and the last end of those who put their trust in such things. It should make us see the necessity of entire detachment from all the passing and deceitful goods of this life. (Christian Education Book III. chap. ii. No. 9.)

In the morning man shall grow up like grass, in the morning he shall flourish and pass away: in the evening he shall fall, grow dry and wither. (Psalm lxxxix. 6.)

22. The salvation of the world is entirely the work of Jesus Christ. Only His Precious Blood, His will, His grace, His internal communications can lead us to our end, which is God Himself. All else is of little avail, whether it be genius, or strength, or riches, or any human contrivance whatever: all these are nothing. The power of Jesus Christ alone can save us. (Catechetical Instructions 24.)

Neither is there salvation in any other. For there is no other name under heaven given to men, whereby we must be saved. (Acts iv. 12.)

23. We are now preparing to celebrate the birth of that Divine Person who came down from heaven to redeem us by His Death, according to the will of His heavenly Father. At this time it is customary for friends to exchange good wishes, and I can wish you nothing better than that the will of God and yours, and indeed those of all men, may be but one will, and that we may all be consummated in unity. (Letters 5754.)

That He might make known unto us the mystery of His will, according to His good pleasure which He hath purposed in Him, (Ephesians i. 9.)

24. For the feast of Christmas, the faithful ought, firstly, to prepare themselves on the vigil by fasting and recollection ; secondly, to assist with great and tender devotion at the divine offices of the preceding night, if circumstances permit ; thirdly, to receive our Blessed Lord in the Holy Eucharist with an ardent desire to begin a new and holy life by His grace. (Catechism No. 670.)

In the morning you shall see the glory of the Lord. (Exodus xvi. 7.)

25. See how poor the Divine Infant is! How He shivers with cold! And yet men refuse to acknowledge Him! Who would not yearn to make Him a return of love, and gladly be poor and forgotten with Him! What are our sufferings when compared with those of the Child Jesus? And who are we and who is He? We may learn who He is from the lips of His holy and gentle Mother, who is so happy now at finding herself with Him in the stable, which is not dark, since the light of souls is there, nor cold, because the fire of charity is ablaze. The Virgin Mother will speak to our hearts if we draw near to hers, she will make us realize it all and share her feelings. (Letters 5222.)

And she brought forth her first-born Son, and wrapped Him in swaddling clothes, and laid Him in a manger: because. . . . there was no room for them in the inn. (St. Luke ii. 7.)

26. In this way did that great Individual of the human species come among us, who was to hold the chiefdom in the vast family of human beings, nay, the highest place in all creation, which, by the bond of personal union, was in Him linked to the Creator. Thus was realized not merely the archetype of humanity, but the deification of human nature. Thus was man, a being inferior to all other intelligences, nay, even what was meanest in man, his very flesh, exalted to so sublime a dignity as to deserve the adoration of all angelic minds: "And the Word was made flesh." (Theodicy No 755.)

While all things were in quiet silence, and the night was in the midst of her course, Thy Almighty Word leapt down from heaven from Thy royal throne. (Wisdom xviii. 14, 15.)

27. The flower which thus blossomed on the rod of Jesse was in itself a product of infinite worth and loveliness; it was a human individual exalted above all human greatness, an individual who was God. Hence, even if all the rest of mankind had been lost, human nature would have brought forth most abundant fruit. The victory over evil was secured by this fact (the Incarnation) alone. (Theodicy No. 765.)

And there shall come forth a rod out of the root of Jesse, and a flower shall rise up out of his root. And the Spirit of the Lord shall rest upon Him. (Isaias xi. 1, 2.)

28. Thus it came to pass that while human nature, with the exception of the

Virgin of Nazareth, grew even more degenerate the Lord of the universe said: "Behold I come." I come to draw forth from the finite, which has become utterly worthless, an infinite good. Then the Word was made flesh, and a terrible war began, not between two opposing forces of nature, but between the natural and the supernatural. (Theodicy No. 764.)

Do not think that I came to send peace upon earth: I came not to send peace, but the sword. (St. Matthew x. 34.)

29. We see realized in Christ the archetype of humanity exalted to the highest summit of perfection: all the other saints are the realization of particular types and species, and have in part alone that which Christ has in fulness, and which He communicates to them without diminution to Himself, according to that which is written: "Of His fulness we have all received." (Theodicy No. 951.)

Who is the image of the invisible God, the first-born of every creature. For in Him were all things created in heaven, and on earth. . . . . And He is before all, and by Him all things consist. Because in Him it hath well pleased the Father that all fullness should dwell. (Colossians i. 15, 16, 17, 19.)

30. We know that the present life is the season of mercy: the future life, the season of justice. Yet we allow the tide of our present life to flow on unheeded, though during its course we have to work out our salvation, and we are hurried on towards the time of justice with scarcely a thought about it. What folly, what inconceivable madness, if experience did not prove it to be a fact! (Letters 556.)

Delay not to be converted to the Lord, and defer it not from day to day. For His wrath shall come on a sudden, and in the time of vengeance He will destroy thee. (Ecclesiasticus v. 8, 9.)

31. Time stands still for those who perform good works which, though done in time, will last for eternity, and which are the only good that time effects. Were it not for this, what would time be but an old trifler, who leaves nothing behind him in his course, but carries away our dry bones along with his own? (Letters 5506.)

Hasten the time, and remember the end, that they may declare Thy wonderful works. (Ecclesiasticus xxxvi. 10.)

INDEX.

ABNEGATION OF SELF
    in what it consists, Sept. 6th. Also March 27th, March 28th, and Sept. 24th.

ACCUSATIONS, FALSE
    how to profit by, July 29th.

AFFECTIONS, NATURAL
    sanctified by Divine Love, Nov. 27th, Dec. 20th. Also Sept. 4th.

ANGELS
    end of their creation, Oct. 1st.
    how they assist us, Oct. 2nd.

CHARITY
    preferable to learning, March 7th.
    habit of, March 22nd.
    disposition for works of, July 6th.
    weakened by party spirit, July 27th.
    towards our neighbour, Sept. 10th.
    how to undertake works of, Nov. 30th.

CHEERFULNESS
    benefit of, Feb. 10th, 22nd.
    effect of sanctity, Feb. 17th.
    remedy against certain temptations, Aug. 21st

CHURCH
>not opposed to innocent joy, Feb. 21st.
>its destiny, July 7th.
>the bride of Christ, July 8th.
>dignity of belonging to the, July 9th.
>cannot perish, July 26th.

COMBAT, SPIRITUAL
>must be constant, Jan. 16th.
>reward of the, Jan. 24th. Also Aug. 8th.

COMMUNION
>frequent, June 12th.
>dispositions for, June 13th.
>effects of, June 14th.
>unworthy, June 15th.

CONFIDENCE
>Feb. 12th, March 11th, June 5th, 6th, Dec. 14th.

CONSCIENCE
>benefit of examination of, Oct. 11th.
>dangers of false, Oct 27th.

CONSTANCY
>foundation of, Aug. 11th.
>effect of, Sept. 27th.
>means of acquiring, Oct. 18th.

CORRECTION
>love of, Aug. 13th.
>how to receive, Sept. 18th.

DEATH
>constant remembrance of, Nov. 3rd.
>God's mercy at the moment of, Nov. 4th.
>detaches us from earthly ties, Nov. 6th.
>joy at the thought of, Nov. 12th.
>life a preparation for, Nov. 13th.

INDEX

Detachment
    from self, March 29th.
    from things of the world, Dec. 21st.

Diffidence of Self
    its source, March 10th, 14th.
    compatible with confidence, June 6th.

Diligence
    necessary in all things, Oct. 21st.

Duties, Spiritual
    fidelity in performance of, Nov. 28th.

Eternity
    thought of, Feb. 9th, March 4th.

Eucharist, The Blessed
    Tree of life, June 11th.

Faith
    duty of professing openly our, July 10th.
    holiness of our, Sept. 16th.

Fear of God
    gains mercy, Jan. 14th, May 24th.

Generosity
    towards God, Aug. 23rd.

Gentleness
    how easily wounded, Jan. 28th.
    towards oneself, Aug. 26th.

Happiness
    fruit of sacrifice, Feb. 26th, 27th.

Holy Scriptures
    dispositions for reading the, Aug. 1st.
    teaches humility, Aug. 2nd.

HUMILITY
> Mary's example of, Feb 11th, May 13th.
> a lovable virtue, Aug. 18th.
> source of, Aug. 22nd.
> how to teach it, Aug. 25th.
> effects of, Sept. 3rd.
> its relation to Faith, Oct. 16th.

IGNORANCE
> when culpable, Aug. 28th.

IMAGINATION
> source of disquietude, Jan. 29th, Sept. 19th.
> means of restraining the, Sept. 12th.

INSTITUTE OF CHARITY
> its spirit, July 25th.
> love of, subordinate to our love of the Church March 6th.
> must not seek notoriety, Sept. 20th.

JOY
> not felt by the hypocrite, Feb. 17th.
> fruit of justice, Feb. 22nd.
> springs from truth, July 23rd.

JUDGEMENT
> evils of rash, March 30th.

JUSTICE
> the one thing necessary, April 22nd. Also Feb. 28th, and Oct. 13th.

KNOWLEDGE OF GOD
> foundation of Christian life, March 10th.

KNOWLEDGE OF SELF
> source of diffidence, March 14th.

LIFE
active and contemplative, March 12th, April 27th, May 13th, 14th.
hidden, June 9th.
interior, Oct. 29th, Nov. 16th, 20th.
future, Nov. 19th.

LIFE, RELIGIOUS
school of perfection, July 20th.
advantages of, Aug. 4th, 20th.
apostles the models of, Sept. 7th.

LOVE OF GOD
motive of our love of one another, Jan. 10th.
should surpass all other affections, Sept. 11th.
spiritual conversation tends to increase Oct. 12th.

LOVE OF NEIGHBOUR
causes us to judge others favourably, Feb. 16th.
must be universal, Aug. 29th.
avoids giving offence, Sept. 11th.
is born of God, Sept. 13th.

MAGNANIMITY
necessity of, June 3rd.

MARY
her humility, Feb. 11th.
our mother, April 2nd.
utility of devotion to, May 2nd, 5th, 31st, July 16th.
invocation of her name, May 7th, Sept. 12th, Nov. 21st.
mother and member of the Church, May 8th.
mother of the Christian Priesthood, May 10th.
our model, May 11th.

MARY—*(continued)*
    her life of retirement, May 13th, 14th.
    the " Blessed " Virgin, May 20th, 21st.
    refuge of sinners, May 29th.

MEDITATION
    subjects for, April 6th, Oct. 24th.
    how important, Oct. 10th.

MERIT
    to be sought, not enjoyment, March 3rd.

MISFORTUNES, TEMPORAL
    advantages of, March 9th, Oct. 25th.

MORTIFICATION
    necessity of, March 1st, Dec. 5th.

NAME OF JESUS
    sweetness of, Jan. 17th, Sept. 12th.

OBEDIENCE
    infallible guide, Jan. 20th, Sept. 5th.
    value of, July 12th, 14th.
    reasonableness of, Sept. 2nd.
    fruit of humility, Sept. 3rd, 6th, Nov. 14th.

PENANCE
    best kind of, Sept. 14th.

PERFECTION
    study of, Jan. 5th, Feb. 8th.

POVERTY
    its reward, Oct. 5th.

PRAISES OF MEN
    worthlessness of, Aug. 24th.

PRAYER
    ejaculatory, Jan. 4th.
    necessity of, April 21st.
    efficacy of, April 25th, Nov. 17th.
    should be unceasing, June 8th.
    vocal, Oct. 10th, Dec. 2nd.
    spirit of, Dec. 1st.

PRESENCE OF GOD
    keeps up the interior spirit, Jan. 2nd.
    witholds us from sin, Jan. 3rd, Aug. 17th. See also June 8th.

PRIDE
    its folly, Oct. 16th.
    springs from ignorance, Nov. 25th.

PRUDENCE
    necessity of, Feb. 3rd, Aug. 5th.
    two kinds of, April 29th.
    in what it consists, Aug. 31st.

PURGATORY
    prayers for souls in, Nov. 2nd, 7th, 8th.
    sufferings of, Nov. 10th.
    a consoling doctrine, Nov. 11th.

PUSILLANIMITY
    June 4th, Dec. 9th.

REFLECTION ON SELF
    necessity of avoiding, Oct. 17th.

RESTING IN GOD
    strength derived from, Feb. 14th, July 28th.

RESURRECTION
    duties on the feast of the, April 11th.
    foundation of religion, April 12th.
    our justification, April 14th.
    effects of the, April 15th, 16th.

SACRED HEART
    devotion to the, June 1st, 2nd.

SACRED HUMANITY
    various thoughts on the, March 20th, June 17th, 18th, 19th, 20th.

SADNESS
    its sources, Feb. 17th, April 23rd. Also Feb. 23rd.

SALVATION
    work of God alone, Jan. 11th, Dec. 17th.
    can be attained by all, Jan. 13th. See also Nov. 18th.

SANCTIFICATION
    our only good, July 3rd, 4th.

SELF-LOVE
    source of hidden sins, Jan. 19th, 29th.
    mortification of, Sept. 17th.

SELF-SACRIFICE
    necessity of, Jan. 22nd, Feb. 1st.

SENSUALITY
    See March 15th, 16th, 17th.

SIMPLICITY
    to accompany our actions, Feb. 3rd, 18th
    to be united to prudence, Aug. 5th.

SIN
> sorrow for, Feb. 24th.
> gravity of, Feb. 25th.
> avoidance of venial, Aug. 30th.

SPIRIT OF THE WORLD
> to be avoided, Feb. 5th, 7th.

SUFFERINGS
> inevitable, March 2nd.   Also Feb. 15th.

TIME
> good use of, Sept. 9th, Dec. 30th, 31st.

TEMPTATIONS
> to be endured tranquilly, March 24th.

TRUTH
> love of, Jan. 18th, 21st, April 21st, July 30th, Oct. 23rd, 26th.

UNION WITH GOD
> fruit of prayer, April 21st.
> leads to desire of contemplative life, April 27th.
> result of mortification, Dec. 4th.

VAIN-GLORY
> Aug. 12th, 16th.

VIGILANCE
> necessity of constant, Aug. 6th, Oct. 6th.

VOCATION
> prompt correspondence with, Jan. 9th.
> temptations against religious, July 16th.
> counsel to follow, July 17th.
> obligation to follow, July 18th.
> love of, Sept. 1st.

Vows
> Baptismal, April 18th.

Will of God
> love of the, March 8th.
> gives value to all our actions, March 13th.
> submission to, June 25th.
> infallible guide, July 13th, Aug 3rd.
> how to do the, Sept. 15th.